# Larks and Leverets

## Wildlife on Norfolk Farmland

*James McCallum* (signature)

**James McCallum**

**Silver Brant**

James McCallum 2006

Published by Silver Brant
Corner Cottage
Jolly Sailor Yard
Wells-next-the-Sea
Norfolk
NR23 1LB

www.jamesmccallum.co.uk

ISBN 0-9541695-3-0
ISBN 978-0-9541695-3-4

Designed by John Walters
www.johnwalters.co.uk

Printed by Healeys Printers
Ipswich  01473 461122

# Larks and Leverets

## Wildlife on Norfolk Farmland

James McCallum

Silver Brant

Hares. One grooming, the other watching me with suspicion, raises one of its ears to listen for any sudden movement.  Wighton, 24 January 2003

# Foreword

William Kiddier, in a delightful little book called *The Profanity of Paint\**, described an artist as 'someone with an inability not to see' - a telling double negative.

We probably all think we see well enough, (unless our sight is physically impaired), and don't need an artist to show us how, but seeing nature through James' eyes we realise just how cursory our looking really is.  James draws quickly and watches slowly.  Both skills have been sharpened by years tuned-in to wildlife wherever he finds it, and to Norfolk in particular.

This is James' fourth Norfolk book.  After the excitement of the earlier coastal essays, it takes a gentle look at what he describes as an equally well-loved part of his local area – the farmland that spreads its man-made geometry of fields behind those exciting hot-spots of the Norfolk coast that are magnets for bird-watchers. The animals he portrays in words and pictures are familiar to all country lovers: - hares boxing and interacting with geese and even a marsh harrier, cock pheasants displaying to their hens, long-tailed tits nest-building and rearing young, skylarks singing and displaying, a stoat rolling an egg, and rabbits relaxing in a wildflower meadow – intimate lives unfolding and watched closely over many days.

My favourite painting is of a 'parade' of six French partridges walking in single file towards you, each bird a character full of wary tension following the leader.  James' line is as perceptive and full of humour as ever and brings everything to life.

James concludes; 'One of the great pleasures of drawing from life is that often you have no idea how the day will unfold, sometimes you never even leave the garden gate'.

Just so.  This is a lovely book, I hope it inspires many to 'stand and stare' and discover the quiet dramas unfolding every day in their own familiar landscape, and gives them eyes to see.


John Busby


\* *The Profanity of Paint* by William Kiddier, Jonathan Cape 1922.
  Limited edition Poulk Press, Heytesbury 1933.

Turtle doves gather together on the wires on a warm, sunny autumn evening. Soon they will begin their migration to Africa but, for the moment, they rest, stretch, scratch and preen. They are dwarfed by their large, portly cousin, the woodpigeon.
Wighton 3 September 2004

# Preface

The natural history of north Norfolk's farmland is largely overshadowed by the richness of its coastal strip. The coastline is justly famed for its rich mosaic of changing landforms and habitats and the specialist wildlife that lives there. There is, however, much to see and enjoy in the more overlooked fields and hedgerows with their more humble wildlife. Indeed it is impossible to visit the coast without experiencing the surrounding farmland. Even arriving by boat it is difficult to ignore the gently rising patchwork of fields and hedges that frame the creeks and marshes. There is a lovely contrast between the coast of north Norfolk with its subtly changing saltmarshes, creeks and open sandy shores and the more regimented order of neighbouring farmland.

The former is as close to untouched natural wilderness as you will find in the British Isles, whilst the landscape of intensive farmland is completely shaped by the hand of man. The divide is usually a sharp, clear-cut line, leaving you with little doubt when you move from one to the next. Once you have in your mind the notion of man's hand forming the appearance of farmland it becomes difficult to look at the gently undulating land in the same way. There is a seemingly endless patchwork of varying colours and tones of large cultivated fields, bordered by neatly trimmed hedges. Here and there the pattern is interrupted by small woods and copses, farm buildings and small clusters of cottages. Church towers betray the whereabouts of small villages. All have the hallmark of man but are always humbled by the broad, open, ever-changing sky and the overwhelming power of nature.

Some of the most abundant and well-known flora and fauna, such as rabbits, pheasants and red-legged partridges, have been introduced by man. So too have the pale yellow-green banks of alexanders, the umbellifer that lines the spring hedgerows and field margins. But these species are easily outweighed by an array of less obvious and sometimes less well known native wildlife. Some species care little for these idealised boundaries between farmland and coast and incorporate both into their lives and home ranges. The to-ing and fro-ing of birds such as gulls and pink-footed geese from their night-time roosts on the shore and open sea to their feeding grounds far inland tightly weave together the two areas, leaving them inseparable.

Greater experience and familiarity with the area and its agriculture paints a clearer picture. The changing pattern of the countryside from ploughing to sowing, to cutting and harvesting keeps you in tune with the rural and natural calendar. A freshly ploughed field in late autumn may prove a magnet for golden plover and lapwing, as does the first lifted sugar beet in drawing pink-footed geese off the autumn stubbles.

Where should you begin to look to enjoy farmland? In simple terms, visit anywhere inland: there is no need for a Cley or a Titchwell to form a focus for watching. Just find somewhere where access is permitted. There are many excellent farm walks, permissive paths and circular walks to be found. The species are widely and relatively evenly distributed across the region. Take an evening drive, a short bike ride or walk. The key is patience, keeping quiet and watching with an open mind, for with these humble creatures that live here you'll have as much drama, colour and surprises as you will have with any rarity or specialist on the coast.

This is not a definitive guide to the wildlife of north Norfolk's farmland. It is more a collection of observations and paintings, all made outdoors at the time of watching. Due to the often fleeting nature and habits of wild creatures, I have tried to develop ways of drawing and painting very quickly, hopefully selecting only essential lines and using simple washes. I have not had time, or for that matter the desire, to make detailed portraits but hopefully the results may reflect more of the life and energy of living nature.

A cock pheasant and a hare during bitterly cold northerly winds try to gain shelter
below a hedgerow bordered by the early spring flowers of alexanders.  Stiffkey, 9 April 2004

# Introduction

I was born and brought up on the north Norfolk coast where, as a boy, I found much to do and hold my interest. The sandy shores, mudflats, creeks, dunes and marshes soon became well known to me. The farmland immediately adjoining the coast also became familiar, however, the vast expanse of agricultural farmland beyond was less known to me and seemed a very different place. It was simply referred to as 'inland', an unimaginative title maybe but simple and to the point. Of course, 'inland' was not the great unknown, as precise areas could soon be pinpointed using local landmarks and the location of parishes. I didn't, however, have the same first hand experience and passed down knowledge of farmland as I had of the coast.

In my early years of bird watching, inland, was mainly somewhere to go for a change or to escape busy Bank Holiday crowds during the summer season. There was such an array of bird life on the coast that frequently included all the farmland species so that I gave the farmland much less attention. With time however, changing interests, values and broadening horizons, this neglected region was soon to hold increasing interest and become an equally well-loved and integral part of my local area.

The inclusion of farmland as a place to study wildlife was an unconscious natural process fuelled by the desire to explore and also to escape the rapidly growing numbers of visitors on the coast. 'Inland' it was easier to find undisturbed places to watch and paint. Increasing numbers of pink-footed geese and my growing interest in them made me realise that I was spending as much time inland as I was on the coast, at least in mid to late winter. This was in the mid 1990s and by the end of that decade I had moved from a rented cottage in Holkham to another in Wighton. Living there, right in the heart of local farmland, I was in a much better position to immerse myself in the landscape and to be on hand to watch and interpret more fully, some of the intimate and difficult to observe moments in the lives of farmland wildlife.

Many regard north Norfolk's farmland as a familiar and unchanging countryside. The truth is very different. It is wholly a man-made landscape whose appearance is governed by what is grown and the ways in which it is harvested. Changes are often phased in and implemented in individual fields dotted amongst large patchworks of agriculture. At any given moment there will be constants in the landscapes so that changes may not be readily appreciated. For instance, round straw bales and silage wrapped in black plastic have quickly come to be seen as typical elements of today's countryside. Square bales and rectangular straw stacks have largely vanished over the last decade. These changes we hardly notice but if we were able to take a series of snapshots of the same area of farmland in each season back through past decades the changes would be much clearer and maybe quite surprising.

Regrettably, 'advances' and 'improvements' in agriculture, particularly since the second half of the twentieth century have generally had a negative effect on the number and variety of flora and fauna of farmland and open countryside. The reasons behind these drastic declines are complex. However, with the benefit of past experience, common sense can produce a very basic simplified summary of some of the main causes. Machinery, herbicides, pesticides and fertilisers have become increasingly efficient. Unwanted insects and plants can virtually be eradicated by means of sprays. Machinery is quicker and more effective so that, for instance, in cereal harvesting there is much less spillage and little waste. Rough corners and patches that were once time-consuming and uneconomic to remove have suddenly become very easy to clear.

Of course, there is much more to the picture than is covered by these examples but they do help to illustrate some of the fundamental causes. It hardly seems possible that within a single generation, many common 'weeds of cultivation' would become nationally rare plants and formally common, well-known and loved birds such as lapwings, yellowhammers and skylarks would have declined so drastically and even disappeared from some areas. At least, now, these changes are recognised and acknowledged. Years of recording, by both amateurs and professionals, from regular counts by local moth groups, to large-scale work for the Norfolk Flora and long-term studies of trends in bird populations by the British Trust for Ornithology, have all greatly contributed to our understanding of the scale of these changes. Such findings have highlighted the plight of farmland wildlife by means of indisputable facts and figures that decision-makers cannot easily ignore or dismiss as 'anecdotal'.

In modern times, can it really be so difficult to keep both large areas of the countryside for farming and also provide a long-term safe haven for native wildlife? Government bodies are having to acknowledge the problems and are helping to make some farming practices more wildlife-friendly, often with financial incentives. Many of the changes are modest but can bring considerable benefits, for example, putting hedgerows on a three-year cutting rotation. For years we have moaned about hedge cutting policies which meant that hawthorn, blackthorn, bramble and other hedgerow species were frequently not allowed to blossom and fruit, denying wildlife so much potential food. Think now of what this small change would make possible: blossom and growth for insects to live on and essential time for many to complete their life cycle; the volume of hips, haws and other fruit and seeds now available to wildlife through the autumn and winter. There are many other good schemes but these new changes and incentives are not set in stone and we must ask how long-term and secure these new lifelines are when funds are no longer available or are transferred to other schemes. Such topics could create enough material to fill a book even without any pictures.

My aim with this book is to celebrate the wildlife of north Norfolk's farmland and hope to encourage people not to take it for granted and give some thought to its future. The story that I wish to tell is about the wildlife that we find and identify within the area today. Occasionally unexpected species turn up on farmland but, for me, the real surprises come when studying the lives of 'familiar, everyday species'.

J.McCallum, Wighton July 2005.

Hare

Hare shapes and tracks in the snow. The settled snow had begun to thaw but falling temperatures re-froze it, forming a solid-ice crust, which covered the fields for many days. Picking out hares became much easier. In the foreground two female hares are lying up in their 'forms', each watched over by a male, Egmere, 2 March 2004

# The break up of winter

A hare runs over a snow-covered field, leaving behind its distinctive track; whilst the low winter sun cast its ice-blue shadow over the field.  2 March 2004

Snow-covered landscape with patterns of closely cropped hedges, tractor tyre marks and silhouettes of hares. With an area of high pressure sitting over the country we experienced a period of sub-zero temperatures and light winds. As the sun dropped below the horizon the cloudless sky turned an even yellow and the hard frozen snow an ice-blue and the temperature plummeted. Binham, 31 January 2001

By late winter the English partridge coveys have broken up and pairs begin to form territories. The transition between winter and spring is often gradual with frequent changes in the weather. Fiddler's Hill, 27 February 2004

Despite the changeable weather conditions daylight hours begin to lengthen and a gradual rise in temperature sees the cereals beginning to grow. Slowly spring begins to dominate over winter. These English or grey partridges will soon ear-mark potential nest sites in warm, sheltered bases of hedgerows. Wells, 14 March 2003

# Spring

It is not always easy to tell when one season ends and another begins.  It is certainly not something you can mark on a calendar for the weather may vary significantly from one year to the next. The transition from winter to spring can often be one of stops and starts, with periods of warm spring-like weather followed by one that is cold and grey or of frost and even snow.  Bit by bit, however, spring dominates, with gradual rises in temperature and lengthening daylight hours triggering a multitude of changes in the countryside. The mistle thrush is one of the first birds to break into full song and can be heard early in the New Year, often undeterred by changeable weather.  At this time of year the old country name 'storm cock' seems fitting.

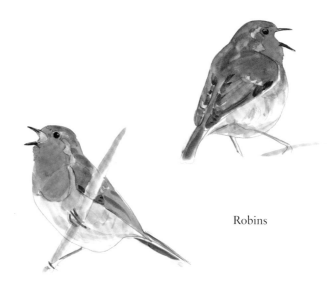

Robins

I find stock doves are a good indicator of changes ahead, for although there is a wintering population here, early February sees a dramatic rise in their numbers.  This often seems to happen overnight with pairs encountered at regular intervals all along the lanes and back roads, where the previous day they were largely absent.  Robins and song thrushes begin to join the dawn chorus, soon to be followed by chaffinches, wrens and before long blackbirds, great tits and so the list of species grows.

A sprinkle of hazel catkins adds a little colour to the hedges and dunnocks begin their curious wing flicking chases.  The pale yellow-green flowers of alexanders line the hedges and verges and the frothy white blackthorn blossom will soon be joined by hawthorn and cow parsley.  Sunny days entice the first few queen bumblebees, tortoiseshell and peacock butterflies out of hibernation.

House Sparrow

Out in the open cereal fields, partridges have broken up from their winter coveys and are staking territories along favourite sections of the hedgerows and edges of small copses.  The calls of grey partridges and the rhythmic chanting of red-legged partridges indicate the whereabouts of the pairs' territories.  Any wandering pairs are rapidly chased off.  Hares are equally obvious in the short crops and are frequently observed in twos, dotted over the fields.

A stock dove peering through a gap in the pantiles on a barn roof where its mate has a nest. One of the most beautiful yet neglected, of British birds. They are very shy and retiring and experts at disappearing long before the observer arrives. Patience and careful fieldcraft may be required to see them at their best. Their neck-patches turn from purple to green, depending on the viewing angle, and can appear studded with shimmering emeralds when caught by the sun. The subtle blue and red plumage tones vary surprisingly in different lights.

Mistle thrush singing high up in breezy pines. They are one of the first birds to break in to full song, often undeterred by the changeable weather earning their old country name of 'storm cock'. Wells, 25 March 2005

15

During February and March we often experience some of the coldest and most changeable periods of the year. Warm, spring-like days can be followed by gales or extreme cold snaps. In the fresh fallen snow the bullfinches' colours almost glow. Old high hedges, tangled with bramble and dense patches of scrub, are important feeding grounds for them at this time of year. Wells, 5 March 2005

Although snowfall may have transformed the countryside into a wintery landscape the hares' breeding season is in full swing. A female turns to 'box' an over-amorous male while a rival male runs up to try and join the action. Egmere, 2 March 2004

This shows that the females are reaching breeding condition and the males guard them closely as they rest and feed or move from one field to the next. An over-eagerness on the part of male to mate will cause the female to turn and box him.

Cock pheasants face each other, their heads bobbing up then down, every move seemingly mirrored until one lunges at the other and they both jump in to the air kicking out with their feet. They are fighting for dominance and some of these fights may last for over an hour. Eventually dominance will be established and the successful cocks are soon to be seen strutting around their territories, elaborately displaying in order to recruit hens to their harem.

Meadow pipits, linnets and smaller numbers of other finches regularly pass westwards over the fields. These birds, having spent the winter in Southern England or Europe, are now heading to their breeding grounds. In the thickets the simple, sweet song of chiffchaffs and the beautiful rich flowing melody of blackcaps indicate that birds are arriving from further afield. The metallic blue and red swallow makes its first appearance on the wires adjoining the cowsheds; for many country people this is confirmation that spring is truly here.

First of the swallows fluffed up against the cold.

These birds have spent the winter on the savannah of Southern Africa picking the flies from around the herds of zebras and wildebeest. Now they have arrived here to build nests up in the eaves and feed on the flies attracted to our livestock.

The hedgerows rapidly move from bud to leaf. Brimstones, commas, orange tips, whites and holly blues have joined the list of butterflies. Queen wasps have been woken from their winter sleep and house martins have joined the swallows feeding over the pastures.

Other summer migrants have also begun to arrive with lesser whitethroats songs' rattling out from the thick, thorn hedges. Common whitethroats perform their jerky song flight along the hedgerows and turtle doves 'purr' from nearby scrub.

Dunnocks displaying

With rising temperatures the snow has melted rapidly. Soon the bullfinch flocks begin to break up, with pairs establishing nesting territories. Early March is a good time to hear the male's very quiet scratchy, warbling song. Having largely exhausted the last of the blackberry seeds, these bullfinches have to stretch out or reach up and hover in order to feed on the last few dried and shrivelled berries. They welcome the change in temperature that encourages the hawthorn and blackthorn buds to begin to grow. Wells, 8 March 2005

The late morning sun melts the snow on
the un-gritted back roads. Large puddles
form on the uneven surfaces, reflecting
the morning sky and the branches of the
saplings. A hare chases another down the
middle of the road. This is a common
sight in early spring, as the male will often
'guard' the female from other males until
she is ready to mate. So, wherever she goes,
he will closely follow; any over eagerness
on his part will provoke a quick response
and she will turn and box him. This is the
most common reason for many of the
seasonal boxing bouts.

Fiddler's Hill, 27 February 2004

Fiddlers Hill morning 27.2.04

19

Large open fields are a good place to watch the spring antics of game birds. Here a French or red-legged partridge proclaims his right to his territory to a neighbouring pair. A feeding pheasant gets caught in the crossfire. This is a non-territorial cock bird; the small red wattles on his face and his low profile show dominant pheasants that he is not challenging them for their territories.
Wells, 17 March 2003

A beautiful spring evening with soft sunshine brings out the colours of the farmland.
Temple's Farm, Wells, 18 March 2005

Despite spending the autumn and early winter amicably together in coveys, English partridges are often involved in heated territorial disputes in springtime. Here two males contest the boundary of their territories and noisily chase each other at high speed back and forth across the flinty field.
Wighton, 13 February 2001

In such contests a compromise is usually found after a day or two. If they can't agree they may resort to fighting. Here two males fly up facing each other, kicking out with their feet.

Sometimes the male and female will participate in such disputes. Males tend to take on their rival males and females the rival females. In this instance the two males are calling and gesturing to each other by standing upright and repeatedly cocking their tails. It is, however, the females who settle the dispute; one suddenly runs forwards with wings out-stretched. The rival pair retreat now followed by the other pair. A hen pheasant and a French partridge watch from the sidelines. Wells, 13 April 2006

A dominant cock pheasant with his harem.  Successful males may be rewarded with many wives.
Crabbe Road, 14 April 2004

# Pheasants

It is difficult to imagine north Norfolk farmland without pheasants and it is nearly impossible to travel any distance without seeing one wandering up field margins or feeding out in open fields. The only exception to this is during high summer when the hens are incubating and the vegetation is at its highest. I first began to pay closer attention to pheasants when drawing hares in early spring as they are often in close proximity. They provided a challenge to paint and, at this time of the year, exhibit what initially seems a bewildering show of courtship behaviour and display. There are so many dramatic postures and interesting situations that I soon developed more than a passing interest.

Characteristic ruffle, jump and wing flutter.

Pheasants were first introduced to Britain in the late 11th Century, sometime after the Norman Conquest, but appear not to have become widespread until the 18th century, by which time shooting estates in Norfolk had established some of the largest populations. Its natural range extends from the eastern shores of the Black Sea, eastwards across Asia to the Pacific coasts of China and Korea. However, it has been widely introduced as a game bird to many regions of the world, particularly over much of Western Europe and large areas of the USA. In Britain there is a naturalised population that is deemed to be self-sustaining although it is closely managed on shooting estates by gamekeepers and in many areas numbers are greatly boosted by the release of hand-reared birds. It is interesting to speculate on how well this naturalised population would fare without this management and annual boost in numbers.

I have been surprised by the extreme reactions, which my interest in pheasants has provoked in some people. Some of the older keepers, normally short of words, can talk enthusiastically for literally hours if prompted. On the other hand, the more fanatical bird watchers can be quite indifferent to them regarding their populations as artificial and not really British birds. Others show a strong dislike of pheasants, resenting the vast amount of money and time spent on a bird that is bred to be shot, when native wildlife is in great need of help. The majority of local people, who having grown up with them simply being there, freely accept them and enjoy their colours and ways.

Personally I have thoroughly enjoyed learning about their surprisingly complex and interesting behaviour and have spent many enjoyable days outdoors trying to work it all out and attempting to put some of the elaborate displays, postures and situations down on paper.

A typical springtime scene with a cock pheasant strutting up his length of hedgerow alongside a hare and a French partridge. 11 March 2006

Pheasants come in all colours and
markings; many were originally a distinct
subspecies but the picture is complicated
by hybridisation. With hens there is
much less plumage variation.

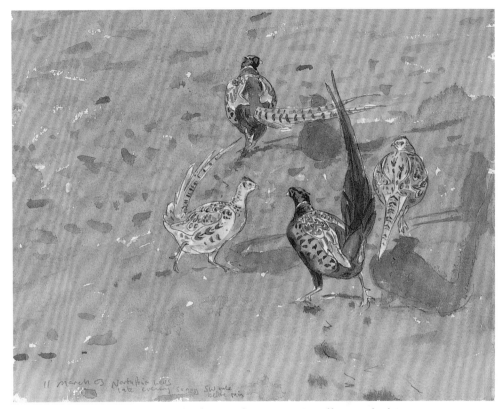

11 march 03 North Point Wells
late evening sunny SW gale
gentle rain

During a gusty south-west gale their tails are continually caught by the wind. These birds are walking across open fields towards high hedges where they will roost. Grey skies and the first few drops of rain mean that they are in for a wet and windy night.
Wells, 11 March 2003

Non-breeding or non-territorial cock pheasants are readily distinguishable; the dull red fleshy wattles on their faces are much reduced and their feathered ear-tufts are either relaxed or absent.

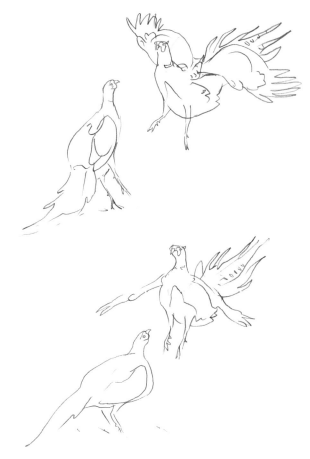

## Sparring, fighting and crowing

To establish dominance the cocks will have to fight their rivals. They face each other, heads low, backs raised and tails depressed. They make a series of slight movements, tactically testing each other's reactions. Choosing its moment, one will suddenly lunge at the other. The defending bird will often jump with its feet out sometimes successfully fending off the attack. If, however, it is slow off the mark the attacker will seize the opportunity and kick out with its feet. Violent fights can follow. If no party can claim victory the tactical fencing will resume.

Some of these encounters will last as long as an hour or more. Sometimes the cocks are so engrossed that they have ended up in the road and I have more than once had to pull up and get out of the car in order to move them.

Crabbe, 15 April 2004

To announce their presence the cocks use a loud double-note call known as 'crowing'. They rear up with tail cocked and often the bill is already closed before the sound reaches you. The call is instantly followed by a rapid beating or drumming of their wings. The call of one male can set off a chain reaction of responding calls. This is particularly noticeable on quiet, still evenings when the calls and wing drumming ricochet far in to the distance.
Crabbe Road, 17 April 2004

plumage to her as possible. His tail, now fully fanned is also tilted towards her. At the climax of the display, his tail is vibrated in the manner of a peacock or lyrebird and he shoots out his nearer wing, dragging his primaries along the ground.

Throughout the display, his head is held downwards and the red face-wattles intensify in colour and expand until they completely encircle his bill, meeting as a half-cap over his forehead. Either side his feathered ear tufts are erected as plumes to complete the spectacle.

As the hen moves away from him, he runs to cut her off and repeats the display on her other flank. This sequence continues several times as they weave an erratic path across the field until the action begins to wane.

### Courtship display

This account was written in my sketchbook following an enjoyable evening watching and painting. It serves as a basic introduction to the courtship displays of the pheasant in north Norfolk.

*5th April 2006*

*At last the cold, strong winds that have dominated this spring have eased, allowing the open farmland to feel the full warmth of the April sun. Cock pheasants strut around their territories, their feathers puffed out, showing off their finery, whilst keeping their eye on their harems and watching for trespassing cock birds. Their territories, more often than not, are situated around keepers' grain bins, no great surprise as this means regular food and any wandering hens looking for an easy meal can be courted and hopefully recruited to his harem.*

*A wandering hen approaches and a cock runs out from the field margin across the open field towards her. His body is now entirely puffed out into almost a disc, asymmetrical in shape as he contorts his plumage and tilts his body to reveal as much of his rich*

Watkins 18.03.06
early morning flight
display

Although hens frequently try to evade these advances, some of their exits seem half-hearted and one is left with the feeling that this is part of the ritual; a complete turn around where the hen is testing his vigour and persistence. Hens, already part of the harem, often behave differently. On occasions the cock wanders out into the field and postures by fluffing out his belly feathers, tightly closing and raising his long tail, then stretching out his neck out and pecking rapidly at the ground. A hen immediately runs over and pecks at the exact place before they quickly separate.

Engrossed in all the action, the time has flown by and the sun is falling towards the horizon as an orange disc. The pheasants have gathered at the base of the hawthorn hedge, which they will use as a roost. French partridges commence their rhythmic chants from neighbouring fields and barnyards. Robins and blackbirds are in full voice in the copses. The temperature drops noticeably as the sun nears the horizon, its shape now lost in a yellow, watery wash of colour, hinting that tomorrow's weather may not be so fine.

At the climax of the display the closest wing is half-spread and the fully-fanned tail vibrated.

# Nesting season - Linnets

In early spring linnets begin to reappear in their favourite breeding haunts. They love areas of gorse or bramble clumps. Flocks or groups regularly feed together and from time to time pairs will fly up to sit on bushes. The males sing their twittering song to their mates. This quickly helps to cement the pair bond and they soon begin to construct grassy nests in dense bushes and tangles. The nests are lined with animal hair or feathers. This pair lined their nest with fur taken from an old dried out hare carcass. The female collected the nesting material while the male watched over her. Having flown to the nest site, the male sat on guard, singing to his mate as she finished constructing the lining and tested the nest cup. I saw them mate several times, the female submissively crouching as the male hovered above her and then landed on her back. Very soon the black speckled, pearly-white eggs appeared in the nest. The female sat tight and relaxed incubating her eggs as I drew her through a gap in the brambles.
Blakeney, 12 May 2006

Warm sunny weather sees house sparrows beginning to construct
their characteristic untidy nests up in the pantiles.
Crabbe Road, 3 February 2005

33

The pair are busy constructing the outer dome of their nest. One bird weaves in spiders' silk whilst the other, carrying a bill full of lichen, waits for its mate to finish.
6 March 2005

# Pudding Poke

Long-tailed tits are familiar and well-loved birds of farmland hedges, scrub and copses. As with many such birds and animals, they have a large number of country and regional names, many of which are connected to their appearance or habits.

'Pudding Poke' or 'Pudding Bag' were the most commonly used names in Norfolk and refers to their lovely oval nests. Interestingly these birds have been given more country names in reference to their distinctive nests as to their own equally distinctive appearance. Puddings tied up in a cloth bag or 'poke' then boiled up would have been a regular way of preparing meals a couple of generations ago. I even have vague recollections of my grandmother boiling up strange cloth objects on the range. The soft oval structures that many country folk encountered in scrub and hedges reminded them of this method of cooking.

There are references to other local names, 'Bush Oven', again referring to the appearance of the nest while another, 'Long-tailed capon' refers to the bird itself, presumably coined due to the similarity of the birds' striking plumage and full round shape to that of chickens fattened up for eating.

Today many people will know them from their noisy active flocks, restlessly moving along hedgerows and from their recent habit of visiting garden feeders. They do, however, have some less well-known and unusual habits and a peculiar social structure, unique amongst all our small birds. In past years I'd spent time with them in the autumn and winter and had sketched them in early spring, building their 'bags' and 'pokes' in bramble and honeysuckle tangles. However, in February 2005 I began an unplanned study. A broken shoulder blade restricted my movements somewhat so I moved back with my parents for a couple of weeks.

Here I was well looked after and could be dropped off somewhere and shuffle around for a while, then either walk home or be picked up at a set time.

Wondering how I was going to get anything done, two pairs of long-tailed tits busy nest building and completely indifferent to my presence answered my question. Tuned in to their calls and behaviour, my slow progress helped me find the whereabouts of almost twenty nest-building pairs in a strip of woodland scrub just over half a mile long and a couple of hundred yards wide. The following account of their activity is based around paintings and diary extracts of one pair in particular.

This pair could be watched through tripod mounted binoculars from the comfort of a small meandering pathway kept open by a few dog walkers and regular movements of muntjac deer. January sees them beginning to show signs of courtship within their winter flocks. From time to time flocks cease to race along and will settle in the same area for a while to feed. There are signs of pair formation, with couples sidling up to each other calling or giving quiet twittering songs. But suddenly the flock is off again. On other occasions one of a pairing will fly up ten, maybe twelve feet, in a strange jerky manner, flicking its wings and fanning its tail, to stall suddenly at the climax and dive straight downwards. Whatever these signs and signals mean, the end of the month sees many pairs established in areas where they will soon begin to build their nests.

February, providing the weather is suitable, often sees the beginning of nest-building although it is not unusual to see flocks at this time of year. These flocks are likely to be made up of young birds from last year that have not yet formed pairs and it may be another month before they settle to breed. In the early stages of nest-building, pairs often come together in the late afternoon to re-form their winter flocks and head off to roost as a group. The timing of nest building seems to be strongly linked to weather and temperature. The following diary observations were made in 2005. In 2006 the spring was much colder,

dominated by very cold winds from the north and east quarters. Nest building began, on average, a remarkable five weeks later.

### 27th February 2005
*Light ENE. Sunny but cold in shade. Occasional snow and hail squalls.*

*Three pairs are actively nest-building and collecting cobwebs. The first nest has two thirds of the dome completed; this was to be the pair I concentrate on. The other pairs have half-completed their outer domes.*

*When I returned at 2.15 in the afternoon, the sky to the northeast is a solid, dark grey. I watch one of the pair bringing in cobwebs and moss as the first snowflakes begin to cover the path and brambles. This is likely to be the last visit the tits make today. The snowfall turns into a heavy blizzard and over the next twenty minutes the wood and scrub are transformed. The light, fluffy flakes gather even in the finest purple birch branches, as there is no wind to drive them. As the northern horizon turns pale gold, the snowflakes cease as suddenly as they had started.*

*The silence is broken by a few scolding notes of wrens, followed by the calls of robins. Woodpigeons were sitting tight and still up on their pine perches, with clusters of snowflakes settling on their foreheads and chubby breasts. They now flapped out to feed on the birch buds, displacing much snow as they clumsily landed in the fine lacework of branches. The sky was now largely pale-blue and, as the first shafts of sunlight burst through, the woods look beautiful covered in fresh, soft snow with yellow highlights and ice-blue shadows.*

*A series of simple, high whistles and a faint flutter of wings sees two pairs of bullfinches bounding in to feed in the brambles, where they seek out the shrivelled remains of blackberries. How magical they looked feeding in the fresh snow, lit by soft winter sunshine. Over the next hour I watch and sketch them. A long-tailed tit flock pass through and I wonder if my pair is among them. The fine snow in the extremities of birch and bramble had already disappeared where* the sun had caught it. Some of the moment's magic has disappeared along with it but, as I head off leaving the first footprints on the path, the wood still looks wonderful.

### 28th February
*Snow largely melted, wind increasing from SW in afternoon.*

In the morning the pair is back building, bringing in cobwebs, moss and thin strips of birch bark peeled from the trunks. Often both birds are present at the nest, one waiting for the other to finish before going in. There is no building after 2.30pm.

### 29th February
*Strong NE, cold in wind but mild in sheltered areas.*

The pair were building until 3pm. This pattern of building in the morning and ceasing in the early afternoon continues over the next few days.

### 4th March
*One and a half inches of snow, turning to rain, then sun in afternoon. Warm and mild.*

The pair were building all day for the first time, probably due to the warmer weather. They were getting closer to completing the top of the dome and entrance hole, continually forming the shape of the outer nest by putting their heads and bodies inside then spreading their wings downwards and cocking their tails upwards.

### 5th March
*Heavy snow in morning but not settling as too mild. NW wind increasing in afternoon with steady snow, turning to sleet then rain. There is no building today due to conditions.*

The main nest materials used are silk from cobwebs and cocoons. Moss, hair, fine dead grasses, collected from the surrounding area, and lichen removed from nearby hawthorns are then 'mixed' in with the silk and woven together. Often lots of cobwebs and cocoons are collected to form into a layer. The plant matter is then brought in and placed on the silk layer. Sitting inside the nest the tits stretch out their head and neck to the outside edge of the structure. By pulling some silk back they weave in new material. This is entertaining to watch as the silk often forms a large loop as they pull it with their bills; this is then attached to the inside edge of the dome, knitting the silk layers firmly together.

Nest-building 3 March 2005

**9th March**
*Moderate NW, occasional drizzle.*

*The pair finish off the entrance-hole during the morning. I watch one of them going up to a large patch of climbing honeysuckle and stripping the fibrous bark into long, thin threads. Later I watch one collecting single strands of silk from the smooth, dead stems of rosebay willowherb. These are gathered in a deft and skilful manner. It grabs a strand from the top of the plant, and then gently slides down the long stem, controlling the speed with its feet!*

*In the late morning the first feathers are taken in; pale contour feathers of wood pigeons. Later on I meet up with a friend of mine, he had found a dead cock pheasant on the road so we take it close to the nest. I pluck out a couple of flank feathers and leave them near to the corpse but when we return an hour or so later they were still there so I throw a handful onto the path near to the nest. Soon one of the birds returns with a large pale, pigeon feather. As it flew over the path it catches sight of one of the big, glistening flank feathers and tries to stop in mid flight. It is so comical to watch it so undecided as to what to do as it flits down towards the new feather, then, remembering that it already has one. At last it takes the original pigeon feather into the nest, quickly darting back out to collect the pheasant's.*

*When it sees that there are others it excitedly begins to collect them one by one. It is terrific to watch the tiny bird collecting these large colourful feathers that covered most of its body, making it look like a strange, exotic make-believe bird found in children's books.*

9 March 2005

With the outer dome complete, the first few
feathers are taken in to line the nest.
9 March 2005

*The following morning I return to find no pheasant,
just a few stray feathers along with the
unquestionable scent of a dog fox. The tits collect
the remaining feathers but the incident reminds me
that I am a guest here only to observe from behind
my tripod and binoculars. Furthermore, there are
more than enough feathers nearby on the ground
underneath woodpigeon roost sites and, on an
adjoining path, a pile of hen pheasant feathers
where a fox had ripped and chewed at the carcass.*

The following days see a steady stream of feathers
going into the nest. Long-tailed tits are said to
collect, on average, an incredible two thousand
feathers with which to line their nests.

### 16th March
*Moderate SW mild with hazy sun*

*Today sees some of the last feathers going in. During
several hours watching only two feathers are seen to
be taken in. Another feather is taken out by one bird
and discarded. Later the other bird picks it up, wipes
it on a branch a couple of times then shakes it before
returning it to the nest. A difference of opinion as to
the finishing touches!*

The first feather went in on the 9th March but
collection didn't start in earnest until the 10th with
the main collection finishing on the 15th. Over the
next few days there is no real activity around the
nest. Cold east winds begin to prevail and, rather
than abandon the nest the pair simply put nesting
on hold.

On the 29th March a pair are mating nearby but
my pair, despite being so bold during building, have
become very shy around the nest site. On the 2nd

April long-tailed tits in the area are still in pairs with no signs of incubation. On the 5th April I see my female sitting inside the nest and later coming out, suggesting that, at last, egg-laying may have begun. On the next visit, a few days later, the nest hole is obscured by a black feather. Suddenly it dawns on me that this is one of her own tail feathers. The tail being bent forward over her head and in front of her face - incubation has begun!

In the case of long-tailed tits the hen does all the incubating; detailed studies reveal that the male doesn't even develop brood patches; which are areas of bare skin which develop so that birds can transfer heat directly from their bodies to their eggs.

### 26th April
*Light showers, mist and drizzle.*

*Pairs are feeding young with various insects including crane flies, frequently removing faecal sacks. These parcels are the droppings of the young, which are produced ready packaged to help prevent nests from becoming soiled and scented.*

*Dots of emerging feathers are already appearing, hints of the beginnings of the black and white striped heads of the young.*

### 5th May
*Cold overcast start, brighter later. Moderate west wind.*

*The young are now quite big and their feathers are growing rapidly; their stripey heads are now very obvious. Lots of trilling calls and 'singing' from inside nest.*

### 7th May
*Strong WNW, sunny but cold in wind.*

*Arrive at midday to find no young visible in the nest. I search the area and find the pair 30 metres away taking food high up into a group of pines whose dense needles make viewing impossible. My estimate of the incubation time was wrong and I have missed the fledging.*

*I follow another food-gathering pair back to their nest nearby but their young are only a week old so I decide to check on a nest in another area. This nest is in a low bramble and honeysuckle clump and is quite exposed and easy to watch. The young are close to fledging and at one stage a cranefly flies past the entrance hole and three youngsters all lunge forward after it.*

### 8th May
*Moderate WNW sun and cloud. Rain showers in afternoon.*

*Young are still in new nest.*

*9th May*
*Cold strong NW. Overcast with sunny spells. Wind easing in afternoon.*

*Several quails calling nearby delay my arrival. The young long-tails have just fledged and ten young are sitting around the nest when I arrive. They look like a heap of tiny balls of fluff; many of their stumpy tails are temporarily bent and curved to one side as a result of ten growing young being crammed into what now looks like a ridiculously small cobweb and lichen pocket.*

*Their parents begin to move them in short stages up into birches and high, rambling, dog roses. Then, finally, as the previous family had done they move up into the high pines. They are brilliant to watch and sketch during periods of inactivity when all ten young come together and fluff themselves up along a single branch. When the parents come in to feed them they either land on the backs of youngsters in order to feed other siblings in the middle or hang directly underneath the young in the middle and feed them from below. Not surprisingly, after all their hard work, the parents' feathers are beginning to show signs of wear and tear.*

*When the adults sound their alarm trill, the call they make, for instance, when a sparrowhawk is around, the fluffed-up young react in a split second. They instantly become sleek by drawing their feathers tightly in and crouching low and silently along branches until the 'all clear' is sounded.*

Longer term detailed studies have helped reveal some incredible aspects of their behaviour and show a social structure unique amongst British birds. For instance it has been found that, at some nests, extra helpers were regularly recorded feeding young. These were adults whose own nests had failed. Remarkably, in studies where the family relationships were known, these turned out to be male siblings of the nesting male. A brother, whose own nest had failed, was helping his brother to bring up the young. Indeed, studies of winter flocks have revealed that young males remain within the area in which they were born and stay to join up with that particular winter flock. They remain to breed in the area in the next spring. Young females on the other hand will disperse and join a new flock. Flocks therefore seem to be largely made up of fathers, brothers and uncles and their wives originate from other flocks. What a fascinating bird the 'pudding poke' is!

Amusingly as I write this account in the heat of the longest day of the year, a group of five fully-grown long-tailed tits burst into the garden. They pause for a moment to line up on next doors washing line next to a rather similar looking cluster of clothes pegs.

Young being fed a crane fly. Their feathers are beginning to show as a series of dots; the beginnings of their brown and white striped head pattern.

29 April 2005

Eight days later they are already fully-feathered and their parents work hard
during the daylight hours to cope with their continuous need for food.
7 May 2005

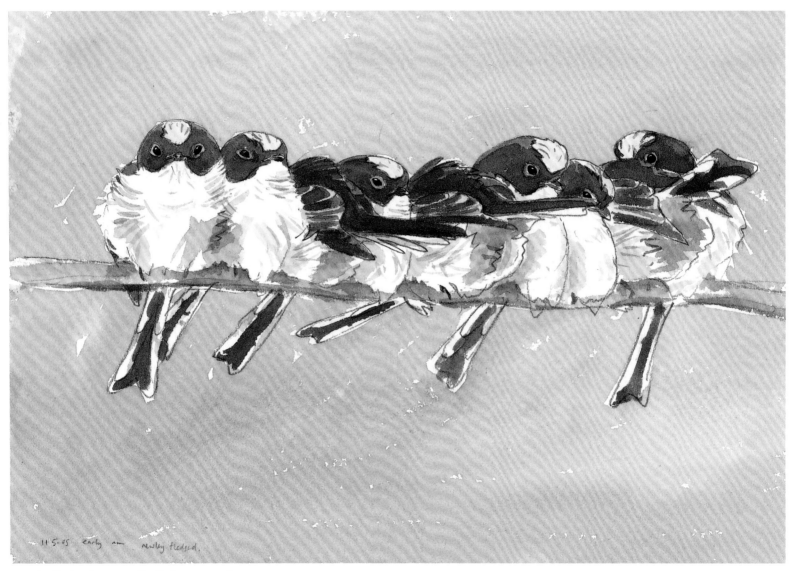

Newly-fledged young fluffed up together.

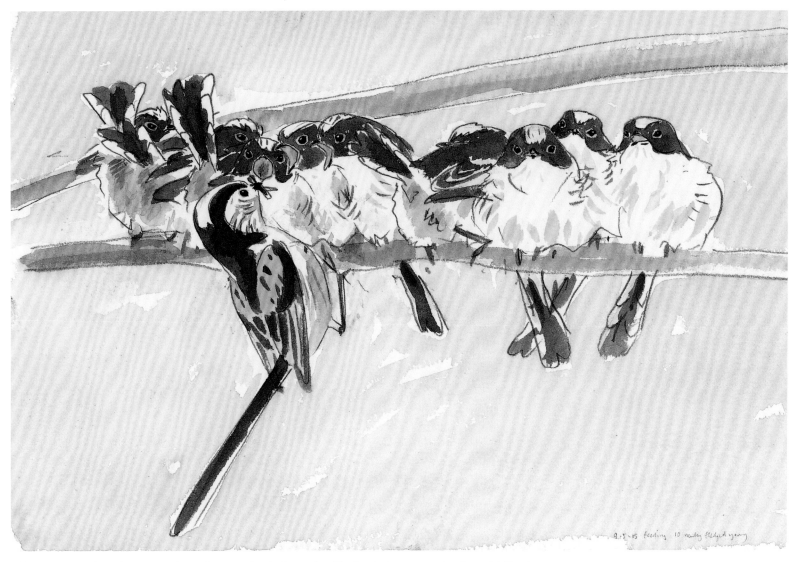

9.5.05 feeding 10 newly fledged young

All ten young lined up together along a single branch. To feed the young in the middle the parents
have to either stand on the backs of the other siblings or hang on the branch directly below.

9 May 2005

An adult hare in the background, a half-grown leveret in the middle and a full-grown rabbit in the foreground. At all ages the amber coloured iris and longer dark-tipped ears help to distinguish the hare from the rabbit.
Wighton, 17 May 2005

# A year with the hare

The familiar hare of Norfolk farmland is the Brown Hare. They are very attractive and well-loved animals and their distinctive appearance, lightning speed and curious antics generate so much interest and attention that it is not surprising that they are tightly woven into country folklore. In modern times there still seems to be a unique interest in hares, even from many people without particularly strong interests in natural history. Most people are familiar with 'mad March hares' and everyone with the 'Easter bunny', which is also believed to originate from the hare. Locally I have heard them referred to as 'Sally' or 'Sally Hare' in much the same way as older generations refer to 'Jenny Wrens' and 'Penny Wagtails'.

With so much folklore and interest surrounding them it is perhaps surprising to learn that there appears to be no record of hares from pre-Roman sites, which may suggest that hares were in fact introduced to Britain by the Romans.

Today they are very common on north Norfolk farmland and the region holds some of the highest if not the highest density in the British Isles. However, over many areas of Britain they have greatly declined and are scarce and even absent now over large areas of the country. They continue to thrive in our intensively farmed arable land, an activity that has been so harmful to other wildlife. Strangely, in other similarly intensively farmed areas of England hares have declined to such an extent that any changes here need to be closely monitored. But, it is also worth remembering that the historical spread of the brown hare throughout its European range is closely linked to man's activities of clearing forests to make way for agriculture.

Hares, unlike their cousin the rabbit, live all their lives above ground. Being predominantly nocturnal they rest up for much of the day in long vegetation or, in areas where vegetation or crops are short they will dig themselves a shallow depression in the ground. These depressions are known as 'forms' and are situated in places that have good all round visibility. When alarmed they sink down into these forms and often all that can be seen is the tops of their heads, their eyes and the joints of their hind limbs above their backs. When in danger their evasive weapon is speed combined with knowledge of the surrounding countryside.

Looking more closely at the immediate landscape, faint pathways or narrow tracks can be seen. These frequently lead to gaps in hedges, gateways or narrower sections of drainage ditches. These are the routes frequently used by hares to move from one area to the next. They know them so well that if danger approaches they will bolt along them at full speed: they know every twist and turn and this allows them to get out of harms way quickly without slowing down.

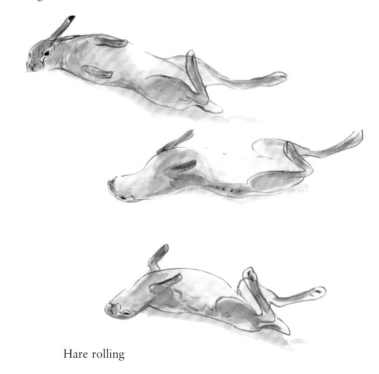

Hare rolling

largely stopped. Many hares could be seen against the snow, lying in their forms. The distinct shapes made by their heads and hind legs made picking them out easy once you had your eye in. In the afternoon the snow had begun to thaw a little, but as the sun began to drop the temperature plummeted. Hares became very active in the early evening and were very obvious running and feeding against the snow.

The sky was crystal clear and cloudless and began increasingly to turn a beautiful yellow-orange where the sun had dropped below the horizon. A full moon was already up and rising in the sky. It greatly illuminated the snow-covered landscape so there was no transition from dusk to darkness. If anything it became brighter as the moon continued to rise. After tea we went out by car. It was 8pm, still and very frosty. Having pulled up at regular intervals and switched off the headlights our eyes became accustomed to the

So, in the middle of the day it can be difficult to locate many hares. However, in late evening they become more active, leaving their resting places to stretch, groom and begin to feed. In open areas, or at times of the year when crops are short, it is common to see loose groups out in the open. In some of the larger cereal or beet fields groups of up to thirty or more can occasionally be seen. Such gatherings provide a good starting point for watching and working out their behaviour.

The idea that hares are largely solitary animals is a popular misconception; this is probably because they are difficult to observe during the day. Occasionally you are given the opportunity to gain rare insight into nature. The following diary entry illustrates such an instance and also some rare opportunities to observe the nocturnal behaviour of hares.

### 29th December 2001
*The morning had begun with heavy snow showers and blizzards. By late morning the snow had begun to ease, and by midday had*

moonlit landscape. The detail that could be seen through binoculars, even at great distance, was quite staggering. We were able to pick out several hundred pinkfeet feeding, a snipe and a woodcock together on a frozen pool and watch a little owl sitting above us in an ash tree. Best of all was the abundance of hares. We saw several hundred during the seven mile round trip. Many fields contained twenty or thirty, with groups of up to six. They seemed very playful, running with sharp twists and turns.

The first signs of courtship could be seen; males closely following females around and there were several instances of brief boxing. One large field contained over 50 hares mainly in one large loose gathering, which probably consisted of several smaller groups. There was much, seemingly amicable interaction within the gathering. Although they were mainly at the far end of a very large field they were aware of the car and our presence. After a few minutes the bulk of them ran just like a loose herd of deer through a gateway in the back hedge. It was like a small stampede. We were impressed by their powerful senses of smell, hearing and sight. The combination of moonlight and snow enabled us to make the observation. It is impossible to know whether such large gatherings are regular nightly occurances or simply the result of heavy snowfall and lack of suitable feeding areas.

The breeding season may vary according to weather conditions but it is possible to see the first signs of courtship not long after Christmas and my earliest observation of mating is on the 3rd January 2000. The breeding season continues until about mid September. Local observations of young hares, or leverets, confirm this pattern, with sightings ranging from the second week of February to early October.

When the females come into breeding condition the behaviour of the males quickly changes. They seem preoccupied with running around, picking up and following the scent of potential mates. They seem to concentrate much of their energy on this activity and these normally cautious and wary animals may become quite bold, running by with head down and nostrils open.

Unfortunately this preoccupation sees them throw caution to the wind and dart through gaps in hedges and through gateways directly onto roads. Many are killed at such times and it is especially noticeable early in the season, as many females will reach breeding condition at the same time. Hares are polygamous and males may mate with several females. Indeed dominant males may mate with a large proportion of the females in a particular area. Males will however stay in close contact with a female and 'guard' her from other males until she is ready to mate, after which he may soon loose interest in her. This pattern is quite typical. However, I have seen pairs stay together for several days and mate regularly during that period.

'Boxing' is the best known aspect of hare behaviour and occurs most regularly during the 'guarding' period. It used to be believed that boxing took place between two males fighting over a female but it is, in fact, the reaction of a female, not yet ready to mate to an over attentive male. In such circumstances an exasperated female may suddenly turn and face the male, both animals now standing upright on their hind legs, the female lunging out with her forelegs and the male defending with his. This is usually a quick bout but it may have to be repeated regularly. Sometimes boxing can be a more prolonged and violent-looking affair with much fur flying.

In fairness to past observers it has to be said that males will occasionally box other males. This usually occurs when a male is 'guarding' a female and another male is also showing some interest in her.

The 'guarding' male will dash after the rival; sometimes this action is enough, if it's not a quick punch may suffice. If he doesn't back off then boxing and further chasing will follow with one of the males eventually coming out on top and returning to 'guard' the female.

Pregnancy is said to last for about forty-two days. The young are born with their eyes wide open, fully covered with fur and are soon able to move around if they need to. Litters of up to five young have been recorded locally with three being the most common. Litters may be smaller earlier in the season, particularly if the weather is poor or the growing season late. Leverets are born in long vegetation where they are concealed in a rough 'nest'. They will remain there together for a day or so until their mother decides to split them up. They are relocated within the immediate area, each lying up in long vegetation or its own form; this is a tactic used to increase the survival rate of the litter. Leverets require minimal attention and the mother will visit only once each day at, or just after dusk so that they can suckle. She will tend them for about three or four weeks after which they must become independent. Females will have an average of three litters each season.

These young leverets grow quite quickly but it will take about another four or five months for them to become adults. By early summer these half-grown leverets are often at their most obvious and can be seen around field margins and other areas where crops or vegetation are low. They are extremely attractive at this stage being diminutive versions of the adults. They also show some puzzling behaviour at this age; they constantly try to bond with other hares by following them around and trying to nuzzle up against them. The reasons for this are not clear; maybe they are not fully used to their forced independence. Adult hares will not tolerate this behaviour and will shoo them away by putting their heads down and nudging them with their head or nose. Often this is combined with a darting run.

This is incidentally, typical hare threat behaviour and its speed and force indicate its intensity. Leverets moved on in this manner will approach other hares and will meet the same reaction. If other leverets are approached they are usually more tolerant and several may be seen together. Sometimes there may be a distinct difference in size and age, so there is no possibility that these groups consist of siblings only. Much stranger still is the fact that, having been repeatedly snubbed by adult hares, I have seen these half-grown leverets trying to bond with woodpigeons, stock doves, pheasants and most regularly red-legged partridges. This is amusing to watch; although the birds sense that the leveret poses no danger they are unsure of how to react, and most of them eventually run or fly away.

As mentioned earlier, this region holds some of the highest densities of hares in the British Isles. Ironically some of the best historical data on their abundance comes from shooting records since late winter and early spring shoots have been carried out on the same farms using the same methods for decades. Although many hundreds may be shot during a single morning this pattern has been the same for many years and population levels have remained high. Although hardly idyllic, these shooting bags may be the first indicators of changes in the hare population. If there is seen to be a decline it is to be hoped that land owners and shooting estates will react by reducing shoots until the reasons behind the declines can be identified and hopefully addressed. We must remember that hares have inexplicably declined in other areas of the country which have very similar farming practices to ours. There are other changes to the area that may also cause gradual declines and these may include increased traffic and the resulting road kill. There has also been a marked increase in the fox population, which preys heavily on hares and leverets. As a result of this many more snares will be used to catch foxes and these are notorious for catching large numbers of hares.

Such changes are difficult to control and can be enough to tip the balance and trigger declines. By keeping a respectful eye on hares in north Norfolk we will hopefully be able to continue to boast of their high densities and populations and enjoy watching the antics of this wonderful creature for years to come.

Hares, unlike rabbits, live their entire lives above ground. They are mainly nocturnal and rest up during the day in long vegetation or they dig a shallow depression in the ground known as a 'form'. If danger approaches they sink low in these 'forms' so that only their eyes and the tops of their hind-legs are visible. If they feel threatened they rely on lightning speed rather than safety underground.
Stiffkey, 19 February 2004

I watched this hare resting up in its form from the comfort of a car as the first few snowflakes began to fall. The snow-fall turned to a blizzard covering the field and largely obliterating the hare's outline. As the squall passed through the sky cleared, the hare's bodyheat melted the snow that had settled on its coat and revealed its distinctive outline against the white field. It was surprising how many more hares could then be counted lying up in their forms on the large open fields.

Cockthorpe, 30 December 2001

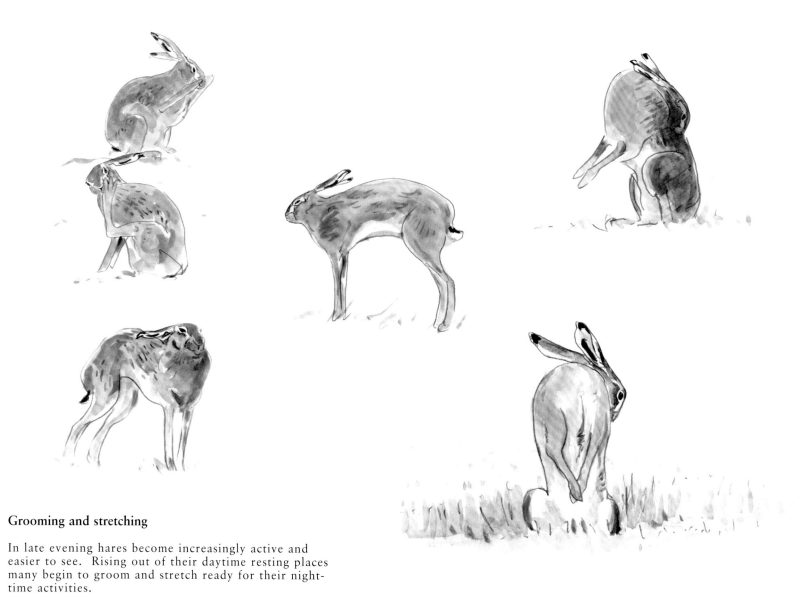

## Grooming and stretching

In late evening hares become increasingly active and easier to see. Rising out of their daytime resting places many begin to groom and stretch ready for their night-time activities.

20.2.04 Cockthorpe evening, sunny but icy Eastwind

Stretching and cleaning in the late evening sun.
Cockthorpe, 20 February 2004

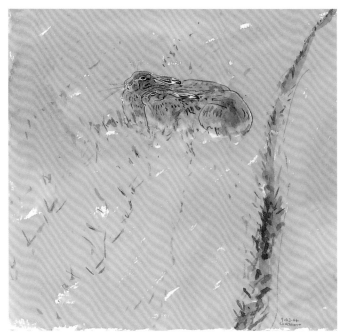

## The breeding cycle

### Guarding

As females come into season males will show them increasing attention. Often a male will guard a female until she is ready to mate, seeing off any other males who come too close. This is not as honourable an activity as it may seem for, after mating, the male frequently loses interest in her and sets off to find a new mate. The running pair were good to paint as the low sunshine cast the shadows of their ears across their backs.

## Boxing

If one of these 'guarding' males becomes over-amorous the female will turn to face him and 'box' him. This is the main reason why boxing is observed rather than the traditionally held belief that it was two males fighting for a female. It is not unusual to see an additional male or indeed several additional males in close proximity. The 'guarding' male will try to fend off any rival males, but the latter can be persistent and will follow the pair around. A chase may develop and, in this instance, the female has turned to box the guarding male but the second male is unable to slow down in time and has jumped over both of them.

02.05.06  Hare seeing off CarrionCrow feeding close to hidden leverets
Courtyard Farm late morning.

A carrion crow continually returns to feed in a stubble field and is repeatedly chased away by a female hare. She has young concealed here and fears that the crow will discover them. 2 May 2006

24.01.03 Weybourn  Mating in stubble with new growth.

Mating. 24 January 2003

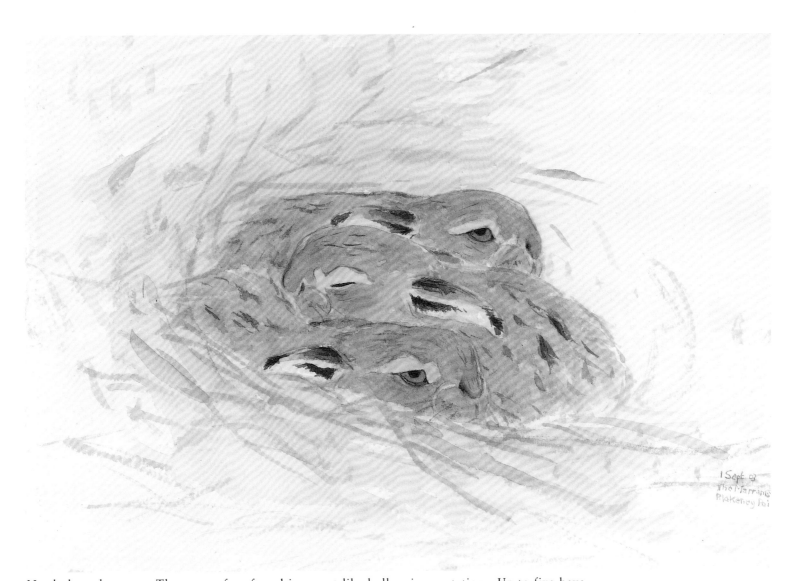

Newly-born leverets. These are often found in a nest-like hollow in vegetation. Up to five have been recorded in a single litter, although three is most common. For the first day or so the mother will keep them together in the 'nest'. After that she will separate them in order to increase the litter's chances of survival from ground predators. The young are suckled for only a few minutes at dusk each day. 15 September 2003

A former gamekeeper once told me how he had seen a harrier take a small leveret. The leveret was shrieking and its mother was jumping up in the air trying to attack the harrier. I never thought that I would witness anything like that. However, one day as I watched a marsh harrier move along a dyke edge it suddenly put its head forward and dropped its legs ready to pounce. A hare ran out of nowhere, leapt into the air and began to box the harrier. It succeeded in driving it off and I figured that there was at least one leveret hidden in the long vegetation.

23 06 01 Wishton dust bathing French Partridge copied by chick and watched by a ½ grown leveret

Leverets, when independence is forced upon them, have a puzzling habit of trying to bond with other hares. When adult hares chase them away they turn their attention to other leverets and even birds. Here a French partridge and its single chick indulge in dust-bathing. The leveret tries continually to nuzzle up to the partridge until it runs off followed by the chick!

58

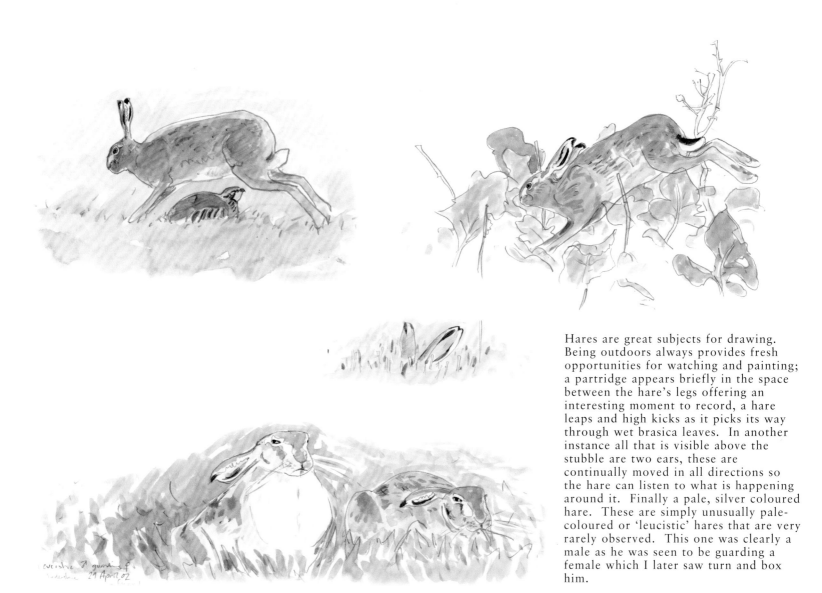

Hares are great subjects for drawing. Being outdoors always provides fresh opportunities for watching and painting; a partridge appears briefly in the space between the hare's legs offering an interesting moment to record, a hare leaps and high kicks as it picks its way through wet brasica leaves. In another instance all that is visible above the stubble are two ears, these are continually moved in all directions so the hare can listen to what is happening around it. Finally a pale, silver coloured hare. These are simply unusually pale-coloured or 'leucistic' hares that are very rarely observed. This one was clearly a male as he was seen to be guarding a female which I later saw turn and box him.

Syderstone, 29 April 2002

## Leveret Suckling

Suckling takes place just once everyday, usually during the first hour after sunset. It only lasts for a few minutes, making it one of the most difficult aspects of hare behaviour to observe. I have watched it only once to date, at dusk between Warham and Stiffkey. It was not quite a textbook situation and, as is so often the case, the observation was made by chance. I had simply decided to make a stop and have a last look over the fields in the fading light. I quickly made a series of drawings to illustrate the event, the wash added when I returned home as it had become too dark outside. The sequence of pictues run from left to right, while the following notes help to describe the chain of events:

*As a hare was loping along a leveret suddenly appeared and darted after it.*

*The old hare turned and nosed it away. The leveret looked to be about two weeks old, too young to be independent, so I kept watching.*

*Suddenly a second hare came bounding in. The leveret, having just been seen off, initially looked a little wary.*

*It then ran forward and the hare rose on to its hind legs. This second hare was the leveret's mother who had arrived to let her young suckle.*

*As the leveret suckled, the mother began to groom the youngster The vision lost as darkness fell.*

# Summer

As spring merges into summer the hares and game birds are quickly dwarfed by crops and become increasingly difficult to see. However, there are so many other things happening that there is plenty to hold your attention. Swallows and martins hawk insects over fields and pastures and have been joined by swifts, very much a species of high summer, being one of the last migrants to arrive and first to leave. Already some of the early nesters such as thrushes and skylarks have independent young and the now estranged parents are busy with, or thinking about, another brood. Very soon the later nesters and summer migrants are to be seen carrying food and the noisy, begging calls of broods of whitethroats, blackcaps and lesser whitethroats ring out from the safety of the thick, cropped hedges. Their parents are now looking tatty and weary from attending to the ceaseless cries for food from their offspring.

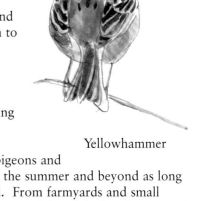

By late summer, after the young have gained their independence, the adults, like many songbirds will become increasingly silent, shy and retiring as they rest up and begin to moult, replacing some of their worn feathers with a new set. Some birds, however, remain in good voice. Yellowhammers can sometimes be slow to begin singing but once they have started their song loses nothing of its vigour throughout the summer. Woodpigeons and

Yellowhammer

collared doves breed throughout the summer and beyond as long as there is plenty of food around. From farmyards and small patches of woodland come the deeper sighs of the handsome stock doves nesting in the barns and holes in trees.

In the taller, thicker hedges and thorn scrub the 'purring' of the beautiful, small turtle dove can be heard; this is a summer visitor whose numbers have rapidly declined, particularly over the last decade. Throughout the summer in the skies above the lark continues its song and, on finer days, swifts revel in high speed flight, screaming in excitement around the village church towers and over the pantiles. These noises epitomise the fine early mornings and, in particular, the balmy evenings of high summer. The songs of field grasshoppers also play their part in creating this summer atmosphere and their rasping can be heard all along the grassy road verges and farm tracks. The 'brown' butterflies love these grassy wastes and can be quite abundant. Meadow browns, ringlets, gatekeepers and wall browns have been joined in the last decade by the welcome spread of the speckled wood, especially in areas where there is a scattering of trees or small copses. The numbers of insects can be boosted dramatically by large numbers of migrants which generally arrive on warm fronts moving up through the continent. These migrant butterflies are readily

Woodpigeons courtship feeding

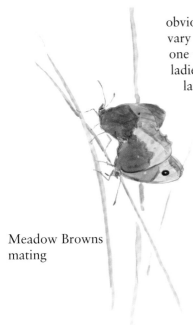

Meadow Browns
mating

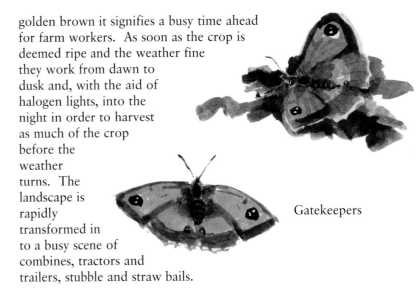

Gatekeepers

obvious but the numbers and species vary from one year to the next. Perhaps one year there may be lots of painted ladies or red admirals then the next large whites or tortoiseshells. Moths too, can feature in these migrations and the silver Y, a fairly nondescript grey moth, readily identifiable by a beautiful pale lower case 'y' inscribed on each forewing, does, in some years occur in thousands.

In the late summer dragonflies may also ride on warm air currents from the continent and migrant hawkers and common darters may gather in numbers along the sheltered hedgerows. Many people have also experienced the occasional invasion of ladybirds or 'bishy-barneybees' as we call them here. When clouds of them descend on the countryside their sharp nip can send people running for cover.

As the cereal begins to ripen and turn a golden brown it signifies a busy time ahead for farm workers. As soon as the crop is deemed ripe and the weather fine they work from dawn to dusk and, with the aid of halogen lights, into the night in order to harvest as much of the crop before the weather turns. The landscape is rapidly transformed in to a busy scene of combines, tractors and trailers, stubble and straw bails.

Hares and game birds, largely hidden during the summer by the ripening corn, are back in evidence. The game birds are a real mixture of shapes and sizes due to the different ages of the broods and the presence of tatty moulting adults. Sometimes it takes time to work out what is what and who belongs to who.

Gatekeeper

Wasp Longhorn Beetle

Ringlet

Speckled Wood

Lesser Whitethroat

Nearby in standing corn are young marsh harriers and the adults busily work the stubble looking for pheasant poults to take back to them. With the abundance of food the young grow quickly and, only a few weeks after fledging, many will begin to migrate to southern Europe and West Africa.

Starlings begin to gather in large groups; these consist mainly of young birds in an array of differently patterned plumages as they replace their predominantly dull brown juvenile dress with a more adult-like spotty one. Goldfinches are also flocking up; the seeding thistle heads draw them like a magnet. The young birds lack the striking black, white and red head markings of the adults. In the villages sparrows gather in their favourite gardens, where there is a combination of dense cover to loaf about and food to eat, their numbers boosted by summer broods. The four-figure flocks which used to rise in clouds from ripening wheat fields have not been seen here for almost twenty years and their absence gives some idea of just how much this bird, once regarded as a serious agricultural pest, has declined.

The noisy, screaming parties of swifts become even louder and more excitable as the young fledge and join in with the adults. Then, one day, usually during the second week of August all is

silent; the flocks have made a unanimous decision to depart for Africa. Swallows and martins, particularly the young from successful first broods, begin to line the wires whilst flocks of lapwings and golden plovers begin to increase on open fields and stubbles. These are all signs of a new pattern as summer begins its smooth, subtle transition to autumn.

young lessers 6.6.05

Young lesser whitethroats. I saw these lesser whitethroats, which had only just left the nest, early one morning as I was cycling to Wells. They were trying to cross a busy road and were innocently sitting right in the middle of it. I could hear the other young calling from a thick hawthorn so I picked them up and put them with the rest of the brood. The adults were scolding nearby but I had just enough time to make a quick study before they moved towards their parent's calls.
Warham, 6 June 2005

Young woodpigeon recently fledged, possibly the closest living thing to a dodo!

Marsh harriers have become a regular feature of north Norfolk farmland since we first noted them nesting inland in crops in 1989.

These youngsters came from a nest situated in a thick clump of greater willowherb in the middle of my local village. For several days after fledging the young would sit in elder bushes and make short flights. The male passed over regularly and dropped food, which the young would fly up to and catch.

11 July 2005

Whitethroats are summer visitors from Africa. A female, newly arrived, is busy preening her feathers. With the arrival of the females the males intensify their singing and display-flights. These lovely, jerky song-flights become a feature of old thick hedges, scrub and bramble patches.

The male builds a series of loosely made grass nests from which he sings and dances around excitedly as a female approaches. The female selects one of these and having made a few improvements to it, will settle down to lay her eggs.

The skylark is one of the most familiar and well-loved farmland birds. This male is singing from the ground amongst daisies whose petals remain tightly closed until the morning sun triggers them to open once again. Wells, 19 April 2005

# Skylarks

During March 2005 I spent several long days trying to locate an area suitable for watching and drawing skylarks. In the large arable fields they could often be quite distant and disappear into the furrows for long periods.

The solution to this problem happened, by chance, on the 25th March as I walked through coastal farmland on my way home from long-tailed tit watching. I passed the 'pitch and putt' course and on an area of rough grass beside it there were skylarks on the short open turf. These birds were relatively used to people coming and going and soon forgot about me, tucked away in a weedy bank. It quickly became clear that this area included the boundary of three pairs' breeding territories and was a perfect place to watch and paint their behaviour.

Being familiar birds, I assumed I would have seen much of their breeding behaviour such as fights, chases and the well-known song flight. However, it soon became clear that their behaviour was more complex and that there was an exciting series of shapes and postures to learn. It would take hours and hours of waiting and repeated watching and drawing to piece together what the various posturings and displays meant. It was nonetheless highly enjoyable, if not at times frustrating.

**Dust-bathing**

This activity is part of feather maintenance and is thought to help birds rid themselves of feather lice and other parasites. It has been observed in many species. With the exception of sparrows and possibly game birds I don't know of any other species, which dust-bathes as regularly as the skylark. These particular birds nested in an area of short turf and, providing the weather was dry enough to loosen the soil, continually visited a series of mole-hills to dust-bathe. This regular pattern was excellent for repeated observation and provided an opportunity to understand what I was drawing.

## Song-flight

The skylark is a well-known and much loved songbird of farmland and open countryside. Although they often sing from the ground or from an elevated perch, it is the aerial song-flight for which they are best known. Snatches of song can be heard in every season; however, it is from the first few warm days of spring and throughout the summer when they are most vocal.

With their sweet song and impressive song-flight they are regarded with fondness and admiration. Watching skylarks rise in the soft spring sun or in the height of summer is familiar to many of us and so they become associated with some of the loveliest days of the year. Not surprisingly, this special combination of sight, song, sun and warmth creates a special atmosphere and people find it highly evocative. They can find themselves transported back to childhood or carefree times spent in the countryside. With all the emotion, feeling and energy associated with this species, it is no great surprise that it has been widely celebrated in both music and literature.

Skylark's rising song-flight.

Many birds have a prefix to their family name to suggest a feature or habitat with which they are associated. Shore lark, woodlark, meadow pipit and tree pipit are all examples. The use of the word sky is unique but very appropriate. Even when pursued by aerial predators like merlins, skylarks often sing very loudly while they are being chased high in the sky and repeatedly stooped at. Apparently this is to show the falcon that they are very fit and healthy and so are unlikely to be caught. This has never seemed to have any bearing on the persistence of merlins on the chases I've seen, which have been very long and furious. With some I've never seen the outcome, however, in all others the singing skylark has eventually escaped by finding the right moment to dive to earth.

Although the rising song-flight is much celebrated, its final descent is not so. It is easy to assume that the action is largely over with the beginning of the descent and fall in tempo. If you turn away now, however, you will miss the final drama, when the lark folds its wings and dives down towards the ground, often in spiralling twists and turns with its feet and feathered thighs thrust forward.

The dramatic final descent.

The song-flight reaches high in to the sky. On landing the male will often stand in this upright posture.

The male reacts when another skylark, lands nearby, by bowing and raising his tail.
12 April 2005

## Tail-lifting and bowing

This is a very common posture in the visual language of skylarks. It is a way of drawing attention to itself and is used in both territorial and courtship displays. On bare earth the brown-patterned back is well camouflaged but the underside is very pale and prominent. The display is used by both sexes but most commonly seen in the male. Once a lark has revealed its position in this manner, further posturing and displays make its intentions clearer.

## Threat

When tail-lifting and bowing is used in a threat display between skylarks the level of threat is indicated by the angle of the tail which functions like a warning gauge. Singing may also be incorporated into this threat posture.

If the rival doesn't heed the warning then the tail is spread and one or both wings may be held slightly open and slightly lifted; if not already done so, the crest may now also be raised.

In full threat posture, the flank, breast and shoulder feathers are raised. The tail may be repeatedly spread and the wings flicked. Singing can become very loud. Sometimes these threats may develop into aerial chases, which again are visually obvious with wings and tail fully spread, the tail slightly depressed and the wings raised in a shallow 'V'. Such chases can be quite vocal too and involve rival males, rival females, a pair and single rival or a pair and a rival pair. This visual and vocal exchange may well be enough to resolve a dispute but if one side doesn't back down then they may have to resort to violence. Fights take place in the air with birds facing each other, whilst fluttering upwards and grappling with their bills and feet.

Threat instensifying

Mild threat

Full threat

The pair, in the foreground, threaten another male who has landed in their territory. They react by spreading their tails and raising their crests. This intruding male has decided to stand his ground and reacts in a similar manner, so the pair will attempt to drive him away.
Wells, 26 April 2005

2.4.05 an. pair seeing off ~ displaying ♂

Flying with tails spread and wings held in a shallow 'V' is an aerial threat display.  Here the pair attempt to drive away an intruding skylark.  The male is very vocal and in most cases this posturing and calling will be enough to drive the intruder away.
Wells, 2 April 2005

2♂ fighting & ♀ in threat flight

Persistent disputes may have to be settled by fighting. In a commotion of calls and threat displays two larks flutter up in the air grappling with their bills and feet.
Wells, 26 April 2005

## Courtship

In courtship, exaggerated bowing movements are sometimes used by the male when a female is close by.

Some of the ground singing and postures can be confusingly similar to the threat postures but the presence and submissive attitude of the female makes the situation clearer.

The male's exaggerated bowing and tail-lifting when his mate was close by.

Singing from the ground.

The male sings to his mate, as she crouches in the daisies and yarrow leaves.  His tail is cocked
and the crest and scapular feathers are raised.
Wells, 21 April 2005

## Full courtship display

The courtship displays described previously are commonly seen in the early stages of pairing and help cement the bond between the pair. Just prior to and during nest-building it is possible to witness fuller and more distinct courtship ceremonies. The male singing high in the sky, suddenly drops to the ground, landing several feet away from his mate. He quickly moves towards her by hopping in a ritualised manner almost as if on a pogo stick.

He now stands beside the female with chest puffed out and crest half-erect. The male calls and sings quietly to her with his bill held half-open and angled slightly upwards.

Male hopping and dancing around his mate.

Male posturing before his mate.

Sometimes when the male stands before his mate his wings are held two-thirds open but drooped and vibrated.

The female remains submissive and the approaching male vibrates his nearer wing over her back.  If she is ready, the pair may now mate.

Sometimes the female may solicit the display, as can be illustrated by the following observation.

*19th April 2005, 8.30am - 1.30pm*
*After three fairly uneventful hours, I begin drawing the female nest-building in two separate locations. Unknown to me the male is singing high overhead. The female puffs herself up and begins singing quietly; she then half-spreads her wings and begins to vibrate them, much as a young bird does when begging to be fed. The male drops like a stone and begins the display sequence, which results in mating. Once mated the male flies off and the female retreats to a grass clump to sun herself.*

The female soliciting.

### Nest-building

The female is the sole nest-builder, although the male is often in the immediate area and gives warning calls if there is any potential danger. All of her nest-building is completed prior to midday. At first several locations are used, one soon becoming the favourite. She makes rapid sorties back and forth from the nest to collect dead grasses, sometimes from as little as fifteen feet away. Having collected a bill-full of grass she flies to the general nest area, calls, and then briefly hovers before dropping down. She calls on leaving the nest-site to collect further material.

The pair mating.

Since egg-laying and incubation was about to begin there would not be much behaviour to observe for the next couple of weeks so I decide to leave the area alone. On my return three weeks later I expected to see newly-hatched young being fed but was saddened to see the small rectangle of grass, daisies and molehills that had held two nests as flat and neat as a bowling green. It seems that this was done just in case an overflow car park was needed for the Easter Bank Holiday. This modern mania for neat edges and 'tidying up' places seems to override any consideration of nature's requirements. I'm sure that modern cars can cope with four inches of grass, a handful of molehills and a carpet of daisies. In this instance it was particularly frustrating, as the car park was not needed after all.

The female hovering before dropping to the nest-site.

The female does all the nest building. Here the male watches from a
small mole-hill and, seeing that she has gathered enough material, calls
to her to say it is safe to take it to the nest-site.

Wells, 22 April 2005

Meadow pipit and skylark watching a sparrowhawk soaring high in the sky.
Wells, 22 April 2005

Watching and drawing bird behaviour in detail over long periods of time can,
at times, draw you into their world. A situation commonly encountered is
watching their sudden reaction to birds of prey passing high overhead. Birds
frequently crouch and turn their heads to one side in order to watch the
progress of raptors more clearly. I am continually staggered at just how acute
birds' eyesight is. Sometimes I spend ages trying to locate what they are
watching and never even see anything. On other occasions it takes a full
minute before I can make out a tiny speck in the sky. Watching these skylarks
reactions put me on to numerous sparrowhawks, buzzards and marsh harriers
migrating high overhead.

# Stoats

### 27th April 2001 Kirkgate Lane, Wighton

During a clear-up in the garden I had moved some old *leylandi* trees which I'd cut down the previous year and replaced with hawthorn and blackthorn. They were dried out now and I wanted to remove and burn the wispy branches, then cut and chop the rest into firewood. After dealing with the first couple I stopped to have some dinner. As I sat on my garden bench a male stoat ran between my feet then straight up the drainpipe, pausing in the guttering to glare at me before running along it and taking a flying leap into next door's honeysuckle. Soon afterwards the female darted past with a mouse-sized object in her mouth and also shot up the drainpipe. She, however, continued up the pantiles and slipped under a higher corner of one of them and into the roof. I never worked out her route down, but during my lunchtime she returned with a further three objects, her tiny young, lightly covered in fur but still blind. I had disturbed her nest under the dead trees.

She had made her new nest above the bedroom and that night I could hear her scurrying around, 'hissing and ticking'. I didn't worry too much as she would be sure to move her young again very soon as there was no way to bring large prey, such as rabbits, up the drainpipe. Hopefully their next home would have a more practical route in. I would have liked to

The scolding alarm-call of a wren captured my attention and that of other wrens and we all went to investigate.
Wells, October 2003

have seen how she was able to move her young down again. What surprised me most, however, was how quickly and instinctively both the male and female chose to climb the drainpipe so soon after being disturbed. They had both used this route before and maybe the jill had already earmarked the gap in the tiles as an escape route and safe house if she needed to move home quickly.

### Rolling An Egg 21st May 2005

I have always wanted to see a stoat rolling an egg. I had come close on a couple of occasions when I had startled a stoat, which had then bolted off leaving its prize behind. Maybe if I had retreated and waited a while it may well of returned. On the coast only a week previous a friend and I had startled a stoat, which left a shelduck's egg behind.

On this particular early morning I managed to fulfil my ambition. I was walking along a narrow path when I saw a pheasant's egg lying in front of me. I had no sooner thought 'stoat' when a female came leaping around the corner, instantly coming to a halt standing up on its hind legs, then leaping into the undergrowth. I quickly retraced my steps and this time decided to wait, but after a quarter of an hour nothing had happened. In a last desperate hope I made a squeaking sound using the back of my hand; this is meant to sound similar to that made by a young rabbit. Anyhow it worked and the stoat instantly appeared right at my feet, then ran straight down the path and, to my amazement began rolling the egg. It rolled it using a combination of its nose and its front legs and chin. It then took it off the path and through some rough vegetation with surprising ease, now heading for a big tangle of bramble and honeysuckle. Here it must have had either a cache or maybe its nest.

A male turtle dove 'purrs' to his mate, extending his throat and mechanically bobbing his head and neck as he produces the sound. In an instant the pair take to the wing, twisting and turning through ash trees and thorn bushes in their high-speed love-flight. Wells, 9 June 2005

Turtle dove's display-flight. As the male glides high overhead
there is a chance to see the striking tail markings and lovely
slate-grey underwing, which contrasts with its pale pink body.
Wells, 2 June 2005

On fine mornings and evenings the males call continuously from favourite perches such as telephone wires or high branches. From time to time they launch themselves into a display-flight, flapping high into the sky then gliding smoothly downwards with wings and tail fully-fanned, showing off their entire range of beautiful markings and colours. Wells, 8 June 2005

6 - 6 - 05
Warham midday

An English partridge incubating her eggs at the base of an old hawthorn hedge. A
fine, dry south-facing bank, which has no doubt held partridge nests for decades.
Warham, 6 June 2005

I accidentally stumbled upon this late brood of newly-
hatched young in a grassy patch in Wighton churchyard.
The hen bird hissed, clucked and feigned injury. I quickly
sketched her antics and made a hasty retreat, applying
washes of colour later on.
26 July 2000

A hen pheasant shading her week-old chicks
from the heat of the midday sun.
Garden, Wighton, 27 May 2005

A newly-fledged young hides in a tangle of oak branches while its parent watches me through one, half-open eye.
29 June 2005

Wrens, having discovered this little owl, begin to scold and this in turn attracts my attention. The owl draws itself tight into the trunk, occasionally peeping at me before eventually flying off. Wells, 12 October 1999

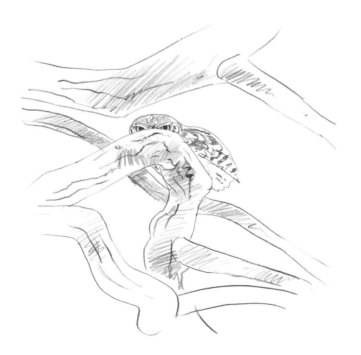

These young little owls are close to fledging from their nest in an old ash tree.
Eight years later little owls are still nesting in the same place.
29 June 1998

**Warham, 30th July 2004**

These notes jotted down while making this painting help to build a bigger picture.

*Some of the first harvested wheat fields of the year. Hot weather with high pressure dominating hopefully spells the beginnings of a good harvest.*

*The hares and game birds are more obvious in the newly-cut stubble. The partridges and pheasants are not at their best this at this time of year and look a bit moth-eaten. They are busy moulting their worn feathers. Groups of adult and young game birds are good fun to watch as they are often in a whole range of shapes and sizes; a reflection of different laying dates or replaced clutches. It can be entertaining trying to work out what the different species are. Early mornings and late evenings are by far the best times for observing wildlife and this is particularly the case on hot and humid days such as this. This morning was no exception and I enjoyed listening to the seasonal sounds around me as I watched and drew.*

*Young whitethroats 'churring' and 'tacking' in the hedges, a cock crowing from a nearby farmyard, short phrases of song from dunnocks, yellowhammers and a wren, wing-claps of woodpigeons and the rasping of field grasshoppers in the field margin. Nothing unusual maybe, but one of those days when it's just nice to be out and about.*

30·7·04
early a.m., humid

Following the harvest, game birds are once again easy to see. They often appear in a whole range of plumages, shapes and sizes, as many adults are moulting and the young are at different stages of development.
Wells, 14 August 2002

Old barn complexes on a working farm are wonderful places. Locally they are predominantly used for cattle and storage. They can be really important nesting areas for farmland birds. This one supported nests of barn and little owls, a kestrel, stock doves, wood and feral pigeons, swallows and pied wagtails. Unfortunately many require continual and often expensive maintenance and this makes them uneconomical for many farms. So many end up being converted to dwellings, losing much of their wildlife along with the charm and atmosphere of the working barn. On this particular afternoon oystercatchers, nesting in nearby fields, have joined the regular cast of birds and 'pipe' from the ridge-tiles.

22 June 2005

In recent years it has become much more common to find marsh harriers nesting in farmland. The young fledge during July and can be found perched in hedgerows close to the nest-site. Here they learn and perfect their flying skills. The male arrives with prey, which is delivered to its offspring by means of a spectacular aerial food-pass. Wighton 14 July 2005

Late summer sees the partridges forming coveys once more. Here a group of French partridges nervously run down a weedy tyre-track towards me, as I sit unseen in a hedge further down the lane. Wighton 27 July 2001

With many of the neighbouring fields high with crops this small corner of pineapple weed, weld, stinging nettles and white campion proved to be a magnet for birds and rabbits. It was a great place to spend time painting and drawing during the long June evenings.
Wighton 6 June 2005

A hatch of summer chafers. During the still evening the mass emergence of these beetles attracted the attention of half a dozen noctule bats and a pair of little owls. The owls carefully watched the progress of the rising beetles then flew up to catch them with their feet. Above them the large noctules patrolled up and down, suddenly twisting and turning out of the sky at lightning speed to catch one in their mouths. As the bats flew up crunching sounds could be heard and the beetle's wing-cases came tumbling to the ground. 15 July 2005

In summer starlings gather in large flocks, many of which are dominated by young birds. The young birds are dressed in a real mixture of patterns and colours and it is interesting to see the many stages between the grey-brown dress of juveniles and the fully moulted adult-like plumage.
Wighton, 19 August 2004

# Autumn

The shining berries of elder and blackberry turn from red to purple-black and the hips deepen in colour. Although the children may be in the middle of their summer holidays an autumnal feel is creeping into the countryside. Tits roam through hedgerows in mixed groups, with smaller numbers of warblers tagging on the end. In the open fields starling flocks have joined together and move in large nomadic groups searching out new feeding grounds. Already some of the groups of swallows and martins have left the wires and begun to trickle southwards. Their numbers have now been replaced by late broods and groups from further afield. Soon, they too will begin their journey southwards.

Hobbies have become more numerous in recent years. They specialise in catching airborne birds and insects. The gatherings of young, less experienced swallows and martins attract them and at this time of year they can often be seen hunting alone or tactically in pairs.

Red Admirals

Turtle doves also gather on overhead wires, albeit in much smaller numbers. They favour quieter areas, particularly where small patches of fumitory can still be found. This flowering plant, an important and favourite food for them, was once regarded as a common weed but, along with the majority of former common 'weeds of cultivation', it can prove very difficult to find, especially in any numbers. Common weeds have been largely sprayed out of existence and their seed banks in the soil, built up over years, largely depleted. Back on the wires, amongst the beautifully marbled adult turtle doves, are a couple of younger birds, less contrastingly patterned above and lacking the black and white striped neck-patch. Sometimes the turtle doves are joined by the big, fat woodpigeons and it is surprising to see just how small turtle doves are in comparison. Occasionally a medium-sized stock dove will join them and the three species, sitting on the wires together, remind me of Russian dolls, each easily fitting into the body size of the other.

Along with their favourite food, turtle doves have declined dramatically, particularly over the last two decades. The reasons for their decline are complex and may prove difficult to address. Not only is there a shortage of some important food items in this

A migrant garden warbler at full stretch.

country, they are also heavily hunted on their migration routes through southern Europe. In addition they have to cross the ever-growing Sahara only to face potential food shortages on their wintering grounds in Africa. It would be an unimaginable tragedy not to hear their soft 'purring' song filtering through the thickets and across the open fields of Norfolk.

Along farm tracks the ivy covering the tree trunks and sections of hedges is now in flower. In places where an old elm or ancient, leggy hawthorn has collapsed the ivy has formed a large clump. Insects gather here in huge numbers to feed on the mass of flowers and the noise they generate can be heard from some distance away. Red admirals seem very attracted to these clumps and during some autumns can gather in good numbers.

Frequently a few commas can be seen nectaring with them. At such times, on sunny afternoons, these ivy clumps can look jewel

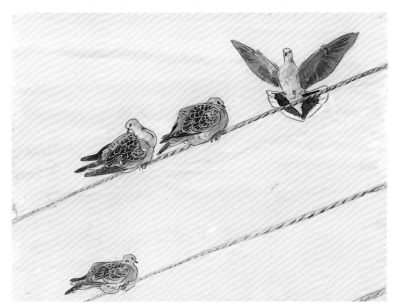

Turtle doves gathering on wires during September, just prior to migration. Wighton, 1 September 2004

encrusted and become places of great beauty. Many wasps gather nectar here too. These workers are replenishing their energy levels following a summer's work of both, collecting insects for the grubs inside their nest and gathering wood pulp to make new egg chambers for the queen.

Warham, 11 September 2004

Here she will lay more eggs in order to increase her army of workers. On still days you can hear the workers munching away at old dry hogweed stems and fence posts and many also show a liking for the cedar trellis in the garden. The workers return to the nest with balls of wood pulp, the basis for the strong, papery nest. The subtle bands of colour no doubt reflect the different origins of the material. As the autumn moves on the life of the nest, its workers and its queen will cease. The queen will now lay eggs, which will develop into new queens and males. They will leave the nest and mate; the male's task is now done and the new queens will hibernate for the winter before beginning their own nests next spring.

On some autumn mornings the first person to walk down narrow paths may have to navigate a way through a mass of garden spider webs. These orb spiders are at their most abundant in early autumn and, on early mornings with heavy dew, the low sunshine can reveal a staggering network of these 'classic' shaped webs.

Common darter dragonflies and grasshoppers are nearing the end of their adult life stages and gather in warm sheltered pockets to heat up their bodies and prolong their lives before they succumb to old age or the first frosts.

The days are becoming noticeably shorter and although it's not unusual to have good weather at this time of year the sun has lost some of its fierce heat and the light has become softer. Increased moisture in the air seems to intensify smells and these combine to produce a different feel and atmosphere.

Common Darters

The robin begins to sing its melancholy autumn song and this adds to the sense of change. Many people begin to feel that winter is not so far ahead and start to mourn the loss of summer. However, in the countryside, it is an exciting time of change dominated by autumn colours and bird migration.

It is the season for fungi; field mushrooms and blewits in the fields and pastures and patches where rotting straw or muck piles have been standing can become alive with species such as the shaggy ink cap. Lapwing and golden plover flocks wheel nervously around before dropping back down to feed; their numbers are building all the time and can reach thousands by October.

Periods of strong onshore winds bring cloud and rain pouring in from across the North Sea engulfing the landscape. This can result in large numbers of migrant birds being grounded. As the weather improves, or after they have had a chance to rest and

feed many rapidly begin to filter inland and clouds of winter thrushes such as redwings, fieldfares, as well as migrant blackbirds and song thrushes line the hawthorns or freshly ploughed fields. A closer look along the hedges may reveal smaller birds including chiffchaffs, blackcaps and goldcrests and during similar conditions later in the autumn, woodcock. These rely on their camouflage and sit tight rising only at the last moment. Occasionally the odd rarity

Waxwing

Great Grey Shrike catching common darters.

During the second week of September the first pinkfeet arrive from Iceland. These first groups usually number about twenty or thirty but, as autumn progresses, their numbers greatly increase. Their arrival is in many ways similar to that of the swallow in the spring as it is a clear signal that the new season is about to dominate. The first groups initially favour feeding on the remaining stubble fields but each night they fly to the coast to roost. Gradually much of the stubble will be ploughed in and a procession of gulls will squabble over grubs as the plough uncovers them. The geese are largely unconcerned by this activity as the sugar beet harvest is now underway and it is the tops, which are discarded after the beet has been harvested, which attracts them to the area. Even before the autumn is out, tens of thousands of Pinkfeet will be feeding on sugar beet tops in the region. Their regular to-ing and fro-ing between farmland and the coast is a sure sign that winter is upon us.

Stoat with a half-grown rat, pursued by magpies.
Burnham Norton, 4 November 2004

Migrant thrushes arrive out of the fog.

may be found amongst theses birds; waxwings on berries or a shrike moving along the hedgerows. On the next fine day the birds begin to reorientate themselves and sometimes spectacular movements can be seen with clouds of thrushes, starlings, finches, pipits, skylarks and lapwings migrating predominately in a westerly direction.

# A resourceful Collared Dove

**2nd September 2004 - Wighton**

Following several weeks of unusually wet weather yesterday was warm and sunny. The autumn sunshine was soft having lost a little of high summer's fierceness. I spent a large part of the day in the garden, cutting back the overgrown lawn, left not in laziness but in reluctance to mow the flowering patches of storksbill, cranesbill, hawkbit, self-heal, daisy, meddick and white clover. Such is the maintenance of this garden, geared more to its seasonal value to wildlife rather than to aesthetics.

Having said that it does look very beautiful at times, even if a good proportion of colour and foliage consists of native 'weeds'. Well at least I think it does and the birds and insects visiting have increased significantly during its five-year history.

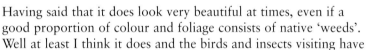

This morning as I prepared breakfast a collared dove was making regular forays to and from a path bordering a clump of herbs and knapweed. Its arrival and departure often announced by a short "hooo" followed by a flutter of wings. I thought little more of it and set out with a cup of coffee to assess the extent and level of yesterday's gardening, hoping that I hadn't been over zealous with the clippers, which can too often be the case as gardening momentum builds up.

Fortunately things didn't look too bad and I began to transfer seeds from fruiting plants to other parts of the garden while I decided where I should bike off to this morning. There was a pregnant adder to check on some coastal heathland and some turtle doves gathering on electric wires prior to migration. My attention was drawn back to the collared dove, which was still regularly toing-and-froing the garden. A lot of seeds had been disturbed during yesterdays pruning so I decided to creep down to have a look at what it may have been feeding on.

Almost immediately its actions became clear as I watched it sort through various freshly clipped dead stems looking for a suitable piece for building its nest. Finding the right one, it would balance it between its mandibles before heading up into a large mixed clump of privet, damson and ivy, overgrown fragments of an old hedge.

This was the border between the drive and open farmland that leads down to the River Stiffkey. It always seemed to be the same bird and judging from his regular singing, a male. He was taking the dead stems into a large patch of flowering ivy.

At the end of July he had nested above an arch of clematis near the front door. I had noticed him revisiting this old nest-site and the ivy a few days previous. I wondered whether he might re-nest in the vicinity, as collared doves will nest in most months if there is a sufficient food supply.

When he disappeared into the shadow of ivy I quickly nipped indoors and grabbed my drawing book. Using a flowering currant for cover I was able to watch his movements with ease. Leaving the nest-site he would fly up on to the gable end of the house to assess the situation, then feeling all was safe he'd give a short call and drop down to find his dead stems. Having selected the right piece he called once more before heading back into the ivy. Each dead stem was picked up in his bill, any not up to the job were quickly discarded and the quest continued. Occasionally, he

would come unstuck as several yarrow stems were still connected to the root and despite a sharp tug they wouldn't come free. Suspicions that his mate was up in the nest were soon confirmed by her occasional quiet calls as he entered the ivy. The male providing his mate with material for her to build with is the normal pattern for these birds. On a couple of occasions movement and flapping could be heard, hinting at the couples courting and mating.

On the driveway a loose group of five collared doves dropped in, they were soon driven away by lunges by the male as he strutted towards them, the bends of his wings exposed and held just clear of his body.

Although maybe not an unusual event the morning's observation and drawing was very fulfilling. One of the great pleasures of drawing from life is that often you have no idea how the day will unfold; sometimes you never even leave the garden gate! During the two and a half hours observation a turtle dove 'purred' from a nearby garden and the first tree sparrow for many years passed high overhead. How seldom these birds are seen in recent years, it took some while for the call to register.

23 Nov 04
Walsingham
Fog + drizzle

Migrant redwings grounded by fog and drizzle.
Walsingham, 23 November 2004

Part of a large 'fall' of blackbirds blown in by strong northerly winds and rain.
Although a familiar resident garden bird here, birds nesting in Scandinavia are largely
migratory and this is the likely origin of these storm-driven birds. Several hundred
gathered to feed in the hawthorn hedges, a large percentage of them being males.
Young males can be told by their blackish bills. Wells, 17 October 2005

Fieldfares are another species of thrush which nest in Scandinavia and choose to spend the winter in our milder climate. On their breeding grounds they often nest in loose colonies where the adults will team up to help drive away predators. In winter they are highly gregarious and form huge flocks, which roam hedges and fields. This flock found good feeding on a local village football pitch. Hindringham, 17 January 2003

The numbers of pink-footed geese and lapwing grow steadily as autumn progresses.
A hare lopes along breaking through a long, 'barricade' of lapwing.
Burnham Overy, 5 November 2005

Rabbits relaxing in the evening sun. Their gregarious habits and prolific breeding
result in a wide range of ages and sizes being seen together.

Rabbits stretching to reach
blackberries and eating
dandelions.  Rabbits are good
fun to watch and draw.
Wighton, 5 October 2004

Woodpigeons, stock and turtle doves. The size range of these species when seen together is always surprising. From time to time you can see them perched in a line of descending sizes, which always reminds me of Russian Dolls. Turtle doves migrate to Africa for the winter. Stock doves can be found all year. However, a significant number make seasonal movements, possibly to winter in southern England. Woodpigeons are to be found all year round and form large flocks in autumn and winter.

Wighton, 3 September 2004

Woodpigeons on a very cold, foggy
morning. These birds chose to remain
inactive until the temperature rose.
They are a very under-rated bird, full
of character and dressed in delicate
hues and tones.
Great Walsingham, 9 December 2004

# Winter

Late autumn really sets the scene for winter and now that the last of the autumn migrants have passed through the remaining birds will now spend much of the winter with us. Pinkfeet continue to grow in numbers and in recent years record numbers have chosen to spend the winter in north Norfolk. Sugar beet is the important attraction and about one hundred thousand, over a third of the world's population, can be found wintering here. They reach their peak numbers just before Christmas, but by early January numbers begin to drop slightly when more birds start to use coastal grazing marshes as the beet becomes scarcer inland.

Finches, buntings and skylarks often gather in flocks on open fields, frequently favouring areas with game-strips or linseed stubble. Such gatherings may attract the attention of local sparrowhawks and, at this time of year, the occasional merlin or hen harrier. Out on the open fields partridges, back in their coveys, and big groups of woodpigeons gather to feed or rest up in the hedges. The late evening sees the pigeons flighting into woods and copses to roost. Here they may be joined by groups of roosting pheasants. Other pheasants, however, may choose to roost up in the hedges or on the ground in rough vegetation. Partridges, on the other hand, will always roost out in the open

Hen Harrier

As the winter nights draw in the night sky becomes an increasingly familiar sight. The constellation of Orion is one of the most distinctive and therefore well-known patterns in the winter night sky.

During a bitterly cold northerly gale a pair of tree sparrows fluff their feathers out and shelter from the wind and hail squalls. 20 February 2005

fields, first walking to the general roosting area, then flying a short distance to their chosen roost-site. On cold days they may huddle or 'jug' together in a group each with its head pointing outwards to give greater all round vision. Their choice of roost-site is changed regularly, most likely each night, to lessen the chance of predation.

As the winter progresses barn owls are seen more frequently in the daytime as their prey often becomes increasingly difficult to find. Periods of wet and windy weather make hearing and locating rodents very difficult for them and prolonged periods of such weather can have a serious impact on their population. In recent years the winter weather has often been dominated by long periods of dull, damp, grey weather. Cold and frosty weather, less common now, is more dynamic, and is usually combined with high pressure and clearer skies. If the cold weather originates from

over the continent we may witness some cold-weather movements of birds with further flocks of fieldfares, blackbirds, skylarks, golden plover, lapwing and woodcock crossing the North Sea to our milder climate. Occasionally this weather may trigger movements of birds not so frequently encountered in the area such as a group of Bewick's swans moving through or small numbers of bean or barnacle geese joining the pinkfeet. Much more rarely when parts of the Baltic have frozen very unusual birds such as white-tailed eagles may spend several weeks in the area. Snow is a fairly rare event in recent years and although it can be a nuisance for people trying to get to and from work it seldom causes big problems. It can, however, totally transform the landscape overnight.

As ever, no sooner have we become used to the relaxed pace of winter than suddenly the mistle thrushes are starting to sing once more, woodpeckers begin to drum, those stock dove pairs have made their overnight appearances and are once more dotted along the February hedgerows. There may still be plenty of winter days to come but spring is certainly beginning to waken once more. Lengthening daylight hours are the initial trigger and a day of warm sunshine may awaken the countryside; the next day may see us plunged back into mid-winter, but nature's clock keeps ticking.

English partridges 'jug' together to keep warm as dusk nears.

The handsome yellowhammer is a characteristic bird of Norfolk's open farmland. The male's bright yellow plumage is obscured in the winter by pale tips to the feathers. By the time spring has arrived the male's daily routines will have worn away many of these pale tips revealing the yellow colour. The yellowhammer's local populations have declined dramatically in recent years and their cheery song and bright colours have disappeared from some former haunts altogether. Great Walsingham, 12 December 2004

Hare shapes and shadows and
tractor tyre-marks on hard frozen
snow. Egmere, 1 March 2004

# Pink-footed Geese

Early morning with pinkfeet coming in from the North through the drizzle, having left their roost on the tidal sands. They head further inland passing over the wet, shiny furrows of a freshly-ploughed field on their way to feed on harvested beet fields near Walsingham. Crabbe Road, 17 December 2004

Pinkfeet dropping in to feed alongside lapwing and black-headed gulls on newly-harvested sugar beet fields. Here the geese are seeking out the discarded leaves and tops left behind when the root was lifted. Sugar beet, undisturbed feeding and roosting sites are essential requirements for these birds if we wish to continue to be honoured by their presence. Burnham/Docking, 11 November 2003

Pinkfeet in fresh snow.
Wighton, 6 January 2003

Pinkfeet heading out to roost on tidal sands. In recent winters over one hundred thousand pink-footed geese have been recorded wintering in north Norfolk. This means that about one third of the entire world population graces this small area of the British Isles. If we want to continue to be blessed with this spectacle we must understand their requirements to ensure that they continue to thrive.
Wells, 30 October 2004

In order to rapidly loose height these geese try to stall the air-flow over their bodies by flipping over onto their backs and making erratic twisting and turning flight paths. This dramatic flying is called 'whiffling'. Contrary to popular belief the geese never perform complete somersaults but instead flop onto their backs one way, then right themselves, then flip over the other way. For me one of the most remarkable aspects of this behaviour is that their heads are kept on a horizontal plane for much of these aerial manoeuvres. Burnham Market, 7 October 2004

Pinkfeet in the last of the evening sunshine. I love these evenings with low, soft winter sun. It tends to highlight the strong shapes and contours of the geese but the highlighted areas have a soft delicate play of light. I find these situations extremely challenging to paint as these light conditions are of such a short duration. The situation is further complicated as clear, bright winter weather frequently corresponds with periods of high pressure, with temperatures plummeting as the sun goes down. Brancaster, 14 January 2005

A hare shoots out across a field and gets lost in a maze of
pinkfeet. Both parties breaking into a panic.

The geese jump up to get out of the hare's way, but peel back down behind it.
This causes a ripple effect across the flock before a relieved looking hare
eventually finds a way out.
Docking, 18 November 2003

Greenfinches, yellowhammers and chaffinches gather on bare oak branches before dropping down into the game strips to feed.
Great Walsingham, 6 December 2004

Greenfinches love game strips planted with sunflowers and
here they are joined by a lone blue tit from the
neighbouring hedgerow.
Great Walsingham, December 2004

A winter game strip. Greenfinches flock to the sunflowers whilst cock pheasants take control of the maize. These are great places to draw birds but they are also very attractive to large numbers of rats and the bank where I regularly sat was crossed with a network of tracks. I tucked my trousers in to my socks, as I would frequently see them running around. I could put up with these but the ones running about and squealing in the ivy just above my head were less welcome.
Great Walsingham, 10 December 2004

A bright but bitterly cold evening with an icy north-east wind. Lapwings feed on winter wheat fields. The two hares sat hunched up and didn't move an inch during the whole time I was painting, appearing much as I felt, numb with cold!
Wighton, 18 February 2004

29.01.05
Sleeping in hedge during
very strong cold· N. wind
c Midday.

Tree sparrows during a bitterly cold snap, dominated by strong, cold north winds.  Having
made a few visits to a garden feeder these birds decided that the best tactic was to fluff
themselves up and sleep on the sheltered side of a thick hedge.
Midday, 29 January 2005

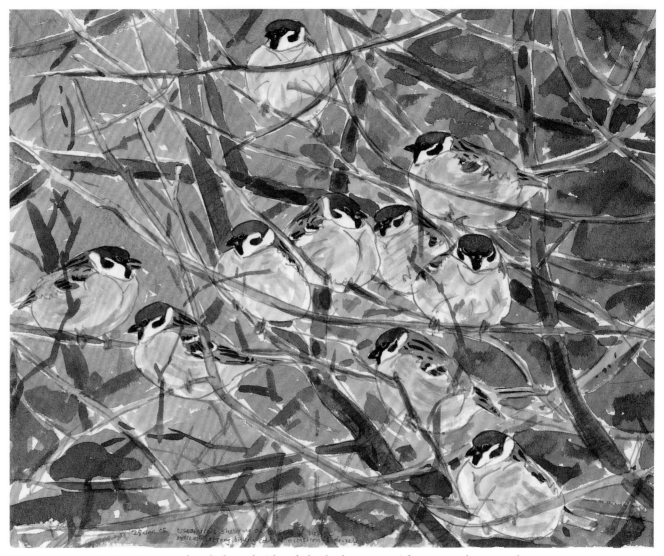

Tree sparrows sit inactive on the sheltered side of the hedgerows. After several years of not having seen any in my local area I was really pleased to find this flock, which peaked at twenty-one birds.
Wighton, 25 January 2005

A beautiful still morning with the sun rising as an orange disc. Frost
covered the fields and meadows, but mist began to rise as lines of gulls
headed inland to feed.
Kirkgate Lane, Wighton, 8 February 2005

Collared doves are a familiar bird of our towns, villages and farmyards. It is quite amazing that, up until 1930, they were only found in Turkey and the Balkans. Since then they have made a spectacular colonisation of Europe with the first British record coming as recently as 1955 when a pair raised two young in Cromer. They have continued to colonise the whole of the British Isles. In this short space of time they have become so familiar that they have even attracted a local name of 'ring dove'. Copy's Green, Wighton, 15 February 2004

On frosty early mornings it is not unusual to see pheasants and
partridges with patches of frost on their rumps and tails.

Woodpigeons and collared doves find a good place to feed in the snow.
Wells, 4 March 2005

On the underside of the woodcock's tail are white spots, which shine in the low light. On another occasion I caught a woodcock in my headlights reacting in a similar manner. The pattern of the spots was so vivid and symmetrical and reminded me of a sea anemone.

One winter I was employed to scare night-feeding wigeon off farmland cereals back onto the coastal grazing marshes. It was lonely work but it also gave me the opportunity to witness some rarely seen and unusual moments. In the full moon a woodcock feeds on a farmland track, it is startled by an approaching hare and reacts by fanning and raising its tail.

Full moon with mist hanging in the River Stiffkey valley. This combination helped to highlight two hares running along the brow of a dark, ploughed field. Wighton, 13 October 2000

Snow-covered arable landscape, the weather conditions highlighting the hares, partridges and pheasants. These, combined with the close-cropped hedges and gently undulating fields crowned with an open sweep of sky, are hallmarks of north Norfolk farmland.
Stiffkey/Fiddler's Hill, 27 February 2004

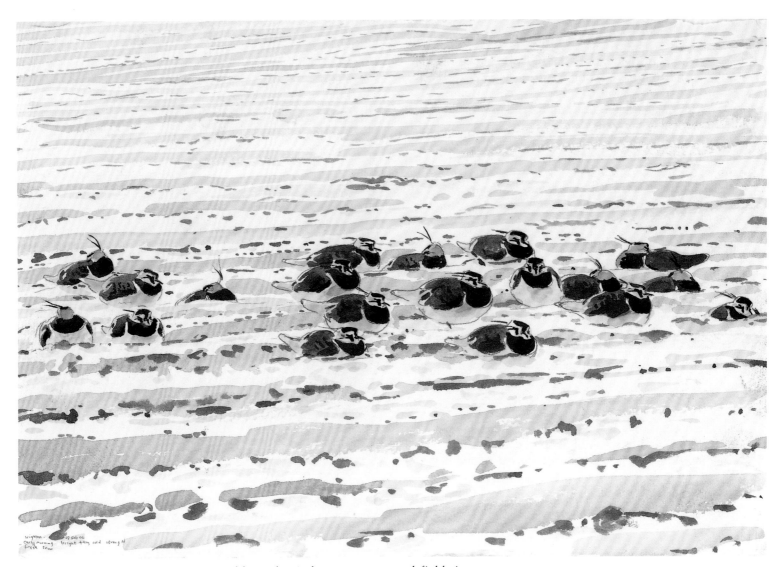

Lapwing sheltering from a strong, cold north wind on snow-covered fields in
bright morning sunshine.  The strong, low light and reflective qualities of the snow
result in some interesting lighting effects.